A Study of Authority

by Billy W. Moore

How to establish authority and how to apply the lessons to life and the worship and work of the church

© 2019 One Stone Press.
All rights reserved. No part of this book may be reproduced in any form without written permission of the publisher.

Published by:
One Stone Press
979 Lovers Lane
Bowling Green, KY 42103

Printed in the United States of America

ISBN: 978-1-941422-45-8

www.onestone.com

Introduction

A lack of respect for God and disregard of His authority is the underlying cause of every departure from truth and every division in the body of Christ. Even though the Old Testament has many examples of those who act without divine authority and who God punishes for such action, and though the New Testament warns repeatedly of this danger and the subsequent penalty, still, in each generation, there are many who profess to believe in Christ and serve Him who act without divine authority.

The material in this book has been gleaned from many sources throughout the past twenty years. It would be impossible to give credit to all those from whom I have learned these things. It is in order to acknowledge some whose lives and labors have been of invaluable help to me. I am grateful to my godly parents who implanted within me the desire to "speak where the Bible speaks," to my faithful wife who has studied with me and stood by me through the years, to James P. Needham who was the first to challenge me to a closer study of authority, to Roy Cogdill, Foy Wallace, Jr., Yater Tant, Curtis Porter, H. F. Sharp, James W. Adams, and a host of other gospel preachers whose preaching and writings have influenced my life.

These lessons are sent forth with the hope that they can help others have greater respect for God and His Word, to have a fuller realization of the need of authority from God in our service to Him, and to learn how to apply the lessons of authority to other problems and situations that shall arise in this generation and generations to come; and that my three children and the children of friends may find help in learning these lessons and teaching them unto others.

— *The Author*

Table of Contents

Lesson 1: Authority – Our Need of It 7
Lesson 2: Authority – Our Need of It (Questions) 11
Lesson 3: Authority – Our Need of It as Seen in the New Testament 17
Lesson 4: Authority – Our Need of It as Seen in the New Testament (Questions) ... 21
Lesson 5: The Source of Authority 27
Lesson 6: The Source of Authority (Questions) 31
Lesson 7: The Source of Authority – What It Is 35
Lesson 8: The Source of Authority – What It Is (Questions) 39
Lesson 9: The Authority of Jesus Is Set Forth in the New Testament 43
Lesson 10: The Authority of Jesus Is Set Forth in the New Testament (Questions) ... 47
Lesson 11: How to Establish Authority 53
Lesson 12: How to Establish Authority (Questions) 57
Lesson 13: How to Establish Authority (Application) 63
Lesson 14: Authority – Generic and Specific 67
Lesson 15: Expediency 73
Lesson 16: Expediency (Questions) 77
Lesson 17: Expediency – Lawful and Unlawful 81
Lesson 18: Expediency – Lawful and Unlawful (Questions) 85
Lesson 19: Authority and the Silence of the Scripture 91
Lesson 20: Authority and the Silence of the Scripture (Questions) 97
Lesson 21: Authority and Evangelism 103
Lesson 22: Authority and Evangelism (Questions) 109
Lesson 23: Authority and Edificiation 115
Lesson 24: Authority and Edificiation (Questions) 123
Lesson 25: Authority and Benevolence 129
Lesson 26: Authority and Benevolence (Questions) 135
A Comprehensive Test on Authority 141

How to Use This Book

This book directs the student to the Word of God. There are hundreds of Scripture references in these lessons, which must be read and studied with care in order to answer the questions that are asked. In preparing these lessons, the King James Version was used, unless otherwise stated. It may be of profit to compare other versions. The student should never try to get a lesson without reading the Scripture references.

This series of lessons is designed to teach the need for authority, that there are two sources of authority—divine and human, there are two kinds of authority—generic and specific, how to establish authority, that the silence of God does not authorize anything, and how to apply these lessons of authority to the organization and work of the church.

These points should be reviewed and repeated week after week (as they are learned) throughout the series in order that each student learns the lessons and is able to make application of them.

In teaching these lessons, I have had the greatest success by spending one lesson period on the outline (in some instances two weeks may be required for this), studying the outline, reading the Scripture references, and trying to impress each student with the points that are made. (Members of the class may be asked to give a brief report on a particular point of an outline. If this is done, the teacher must make assignments in advance.) Then a lesson period is devoted to the questions and answers. Do not fear that there will be too much repetition. Repetition is needed and helps the student learn the lessons and remember them. The material is sufficient for six months of study.

Lesson 1

Authority – Our Need of It

INTRODUCTION

1. Men recognize a need for authority in the home, school, business, and nation; surely it is needed in religion.

2. The word authority is translated from the Greek word *exousia* and has undergone a change in meaning.

   a. *Exousia* . . . denotes authority (from the impersonal verb *exesiti*, "it is lawful"). From the meaning of "leave or permission," or liberty of doing as one pleases, it passed to that of the "ability or strength with which one is endued," then to that of the "power of authority," the right to exercise power, e.g., Matt. 9:6; 21:23; 2 Cor. 10:8; or "the power of rule or government," the power of one whose will and commands must be obeyed by others, e.g., Matt. 28:18; John 17:2; Jude 25 (*Vine's Complete Expository Dictionary of Old and New Testament Words*, Vine, p. 45).

   b. Joseph Henry Thayer gives four definitions of the word, which show the changes mentioned by Mr. Vine:

      i. "Power of choice, liberty of doing as one pleases; leave or permission"

      ii. "Physical and mental power; the ability or strength with which one is endued, which he either possesses or exercises"

      iii. "The power of authority (influence) and of right: Matt. 21:23"

      iv "The power of rule or government (the power of him whose will and commands must be submitted to by others and obeyed, [generally translated authority]); . . . Matt. 28:18" (*Thayer's Greek-English Lexicon*, p. 225)

   c. "1. the power to enforce obedience; right to command or act; 2. a person who has such power or right. 3. an influence that creates respect and confidence" (*The World Book Dictionary*).

- d. "Legal rightful power; a right to command or to act; dominion; jurisdiction" (*Webster's Collegiate Dictionary*).
3. To act with authority simply means that one has jurisdiction, or that he acts by the order or instruction of one who has legal or rightful power.
4. We must recognize the need for authority and have respect for authority once it has been established.

I. Man's Need for Authority in the Religious Realm
   A. The chief priest and elders of the Jews recognize the need for authority.
      1. They ask Jesus, "By what authority are you doing these things? And who gave you this authority?" (Matt. 21:23, NKJV). Note the 3rd definition given by Thayer, see Introduction.
         a. Their question shows two things:
            i. Their recognition of a need for authority in religion.
            ii. That such authority must come from one who has the rightful power to grant it: "Who gave you this authority?"
      2. Jesus answers them with the question, "The baptism of John—where was it from? From heaven or from men?" (Matt. 21:25, NKJV)
         a. His answer shows that there are only two sources of authority—i.e., heaven and men; divine and human.
         b. This is still true.
   B. Some deny that authority from God is needed for all that man does in religion.
      1. This is the attitude of those who either:
         a. Look to self as authority (cf. Jer. 10:23; Prov. 14:12)
         b. Or look to other men (cf. Col. 2:20-22; Matt. 15:9)
      2. This attitude has permeated the Lord's church in this generation.
         a. Practices have been inaugurated for which no scriptural authority exists, and the cry has gone forth, "We do not need authority for everything we do."

b. This is the very opposite of the plea we have made with the denominational world in years past when we called for book, chapter, and verse for all things. We asked for a "thus saith the Lord."
    3. Failure to recognize the need for authority in religion shows that we have failed to learn a basic Bible principle governing acceptability with God.
        a. We may act without authority from God, but we cannot do so and have God's approval and fellowship (2 John 9-11).
II. Old Testament Examples Illustrate the Need for Divine Authority
    A. Cain and Abel (Gen. 4)
        1. Abel acts by the authority of God (cf. Heb. 11:4; Rom. 10:17, NKJV).
            a. He acts "by faith," and faith comes by hearing "the Word of God," therefore we know that God told him what to offer.
        2. Cain rejects that which God commands and substitutes his own will.
            a. He is not the rightful one to authorize his sacrifice; therefore, God rejects him.
            b. God does not respect his sacrifice because it was not what God had commanded.
    B. Nadab and Abihu act without authority from God when they offer strange fire. (Lev. 10:1-2. This strange fire is a fire other than that which God had authorized.)
        1. Note, "which he commanded them not" (v. 1).
            a. They are to get coals of fire form off the altar before the Lord (Lev. 16:12).
        2. This shows that they have no jurisdiction, orders or instruction, or legal or rightful power for the fire they used.
            a They probably think they do not need it!
            b. Remember, to act with authority simply means that one has jurisdiction or that he acts by the orders or instruction of one who has the rightful power.

- C. Uzziah acts without divine authority in wanting to burn incense to the Lord (2 Chron. 26:16-20; Ex. 30:1-10).
    1. Burning incense was a good work, one that God had authorized, but it was one that was "not for you, Uzziah, to burn incense to the Lord" (v. 18).
    2. Divine authority authorized only the priests to burn incense (Ex. 30:1-10).
    3. When Uzziah turns from divine authority, he becomes a source of authority unto himself.
        a. He is not the rightful one to authorize this act.

CONCLUSION

1. In this lesson we have been concerned with determining what authority is and in showing man's need for authority in religion.
2. Those who scorn the need for authority overlook one of the basic lessons taught in the Old Testament and flirt with danger in so doing.
3. The things written before "were written for our learning" (Rom. 15:4). Let us learn from these examples the need for divine authority for everything we do in religion.

Authority – Our Need of It (Questions)

Lesson 2

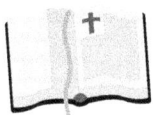 **WHAT DOES THE SCRIPTURE SAY?**

References: Matt. 21:23-24; Matt. 21:25-27; Prov. 14:12; Matt. 15:9; 2 John 9-11; Heb. 11:4; Rom. 10:17; Lev. 10:1-2; Lev. 16:12; 2 Chron. 26:16-20; Ex. 30:1-7; Rom. 14:4; Jer. 10:23; Col. 2:20-22

1. "By what _____ doest thou _____? and who _____ thee this authority?"

2. "The baptism of _____ whence was it: from _____ or of _____?"

3. "There is a _____ which seemeth right unto a man, but the end thereof are the _____ of _____."

4. "But in _____ do they worship me, teaching for _____ the _____ of men."

5. "Whosoever _____ and abideth not in the _____ of Christ, hath not _____."

6. "By faith _____ offered unto _____ a more excellent _____ than _____, by which he obtained witness that he was _____."

7. "So them faith cometh by _____ and _____ by the word of God."

8. "And Nadab and Abihu, the sons of _____, took either of them his _____ and put fire therein, and put incense thereon, and offered _____ _____ before the Lord, which he _____ them not."

9. "And he shall take a _____ full of _____ coals of fire from off the _____ before the Lord."

10. "If appertaineth not unto thee, Uzziah, to _____ _____ unto the Lord, but to the _____ the sons of Aaron, that are consecrated to burn incense."

11. "And Aaron shall _____ thereon sweet incense every _____ when he dresseth the lamps, he shall burn incense upon it."

12. "For whatsoever things were written _____ were written for our _____ that we through patience and comfort of the _____ might have hope."

BRIEF ANSWERS

1. What does authority mean? _____
   _____

2. What two things must we recognize concerning authority?

   a. _____

   b. _____

3. Those who deny that they need authority from God for the things men do in religion are either looking to _____ or to _____ for authority.

4. Jeremiah the prophet says, "O Lord, I know," what? _____
   _____

5. Jesus teaches that "teaching for [doctrine] the commandments of men" makes our worship vain (Matt. 15:9). What does this mean?
   _____

6. What are the two sources of authority? _____

TALK TIME — DISCUSSION

1. Read Matthew 21:23-27.

LESSON 2 Authority – Our Need of It (Questions) 13

    a. Show that the Jews and Jesus recognize the need of authority. _____

    b. Does the Lord and those Jews recognize that authority must come from the right source? How do you know? _____

    c. How does the answer of Jesus silence them? _____

2. Study these two passages: Matthew 15:9 and Colossians 2:20-22.

    a. What should be the attitude we hold toward the commandments of men? _____

    b. Why? _____

3. Why does God have respect unto Abel's offering but not unto Cain's offering? _____

    a. What should we learn from this? _____

4. After reading Leviticus 10:1-2, be able to tell why Nadab and Abihu are killed.

    a. Did the fire which they used burn the incense as well as other fire would have? _____

    b. Did the incense smell the same when burned by the "strange fire" which they used as it would had they used the fire God commanded? _____

    c. Why are they killed? _____

5. Read 2 Chronicles 26:16-21.

    a. What is the sin of Uzziah? _____

    b. Why does he commit this sin? _____

    c. What should we learn from this incident? _____

6. Romans 15:4 says, "Whatsoever things were written aforetime were written for our learning."

   a. Can you see a common lesson that is taught in the Old Testament accounts of Cain and Abel, Nadab and Abihu, and Uzziah and the incense? _____ What is the lesson? _____
   _____

THINK! "THINK ON THESE THINGS"

1. Since the Genesis 4 account of Cain and Abel does not mention the kind of sacrifice they were to make, how do we know God told them what to offer? Read Hebrews 11:4; Romans 10:17; and Acts 10:34. THINK! _____
   _____

   Since God did not authorize Cain's sacrifice, by whose authority does he offer it? THINK! _____

2. Knowing that God destroys Nadab and Abihu for using a fire "which he commanded them not," should we conclude that He will be pleased if we do things which He has not commanded (Lev. 10:1)? _____ By whose authority did they use "strange fire"? _____

3. Nadab and Abihu were priests, thus were the right men to burn incense; they were burning incense, thus were doing the right thing, yet were rejected. Why? THINK! _____
   _____

4. Uzziah, the king, goes into the temple (the right place); to burn incense (the right thing); to the Lord (the right object); but he is rejected. Why? THINK! _____
   _____

   Had the Lord commanded who should burn incense (See Ex. 30:7; Num. 16:40.)? THINK! _____

5. When the Lord tells us what to do, is it necessary for Him to tell us what not to do? THINK! _____ When the Lord tells men

LESSON 2 Authority – Our Need of It (Questions)

where to do a certain thing, must He tell them where not to do it? THINK! _____ When God tells us how to do something, does it matter how we do it? THINK! _____

✓ ✗ TRUE OR FALSE

1. Cain's offering is rejected because it is not as valuable as Abel's. _____
2. God did not tell Cain and Abel what to offer. _____
3. Nadab and Abihu offer strange fire which God commanded them not. _____
4. Uzziah is the high priest in Judah. _____
5. Man must have authority from God for all that he does. _____

🎓 WHAT YOU SHOULD LEARN FROM THIS LESSON

1. We must have authority for all things we do.
2. There are two sources of authority—divine and human.
3. "It is not in man that walketh to direct his steps" (Jer. 10:23).
4. We may worship God and still be wrong.
5. A thing is not right in worship just because we think it is right.
6. When God tells us what to do it is not necessary for Him to tell us what we should not do.

16 A Study of Authority

Lesson 3

Authority – Our Need of It as Seen in the New Testament

INTRODUCTION

1. Authority is legal or rightful power; a right to command or to act; dominion; jurisdiction.
2. There are only two sources of authority: divine and human (heaven and men).
   a. Jesus recognizes this (Matt. 21:23-27).
3. In the last lesson we learned the need of authority as seen in the Old Testament. Examples:
   a. Cain and Abel
   b. Nadab and Abihu
   c. Uzziah, King of Israel
4. In this lesson we shall see the need of authority as seen in the New Testament.

I. Jesus Recognizes and Teaches the Need of Authority
   A. Workers of iniquity will be rejected (Matt. 7:21-23).
      1. "Iniquity" means "lawlessness" (cf. NKJV and NASB).
         a. To work lawlessness is to work without authority.
      2. The workers of iniquity shall be (See Matt. 13:41-42.) . . .
         a. Gathered "out of [the] kingdom."
            i. Not every member of the church recognizes the importance of respecting divine authority.
         b. Cast into a furnace of fire.
            i. Place of eternal torment
            ii. Note others who shall be there (Rev. 21:8).
      3. The apostasy is called "the mystery of iniquity" (2 Thess. 2:7).

          a. This apostasy results from a lack of respect for divine authority. (cf. 1 Tim. 4:1) "Some shall depart from the faith."
    4. Note: When one rejects divine authority, he will substitute the authority of men, others, or self.
  B. Parable of the wise and foolish builders (Matt. 7:24-27)
    1. The "wise man" is he who hears and DOES the will of the Lord.
          a. He acts as the Lord authorizes.
    2. The "foolish man" is one who hears but DOES NOT obey.
          a. He may call Jesus, "Lord, Lord," but he refuses to do what Jesus has authorized (See Luke 6:46.).
  C. The baptism of John (Matt. 21:23-27)
    1. Jesus asks, "The baptism of John, whence was it? from heaven, or of men?"
    2. This shows . .
          a. That Jesus recognizes the need of authority.
          b. That the Jews recognizes the need of authority.

II. The Apostles Teach the Need of Authority
  A. The appeal for unity (Phil. 3:16; 1 Cor. 1:10)
    1. We cannot have unity without abiding by the same rule and speaking the same things, and this cannot be done without recognizing a standard of authority for governing us.
          a. Illustration: Merchants practice unity in weights and measures because they recognize the same rule as authority.
          b. Illustration: Postal clerks recognize the same rule.
  B. "Do all in the name of the Lord Jesus" (Col. 3:17).
    1. "In the name of" in this text means "by the authority of."
  C. We must not "think of men above that which is written" (1 Cor. 4:6).
    1. This emphasizes the need of authority.

D. We must abide in the doctrine of Christ (2 John 9-11).
   1. To abide in the doctrine shows respect for the authority of Christ.
   2. For one to transgress the doctrine of Christ shows a lack of respect for His authority. As a result, he "hath not God"—i.e., he no longer has fellowship with the Father or the Son.
E. Must not add to or take from the Word (Rev. 22:18-19)
   1. Adding to or taking from the Word shows a lack of respect for the authority of Him from whom the Word has come.

CONCLUSION

1. The Lord and His apostles teach the need of authority.
2. Let us recognize this need.
3. Those who say, "We do not need authority for all that we do," have missed a basic principle governing our relationship with God.

Authority – Our Need of It as Seen in the New Testament (Questions)

Lesson 4

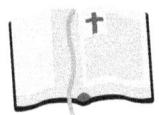 **WHAT DOES THE SCRIPTURE SAY?**

References: Matt. 7:21-23, 28; Matt. 13:41-42; Matt. 21:23-27; Phil. 3:16; 1 Cor. 4:6; Col. 3:17; 2 John 9-11; Rev. 22:18

1. Jesus taught "as one having _____, and not as the _____."

2. "The son of man shall send forth his _____ ___, and they shall gather out of his _____ all things that _____, and them which do _____."

3. "The baptism of John, whence was it from _____ or of _____?"

4. Paul says, "Let us _____ by the _____ _____ let us mind the _____ things."

5. God charges us "not to think of _____ above that which is _____."

6. "And whatsoever ye _____ in _____ or _____ do _____ in the name of the _____."

7. "For he that _____ him God _____ is partaker of his _____ deeds."

8. "If any man shall _____ _____ these _____, God shall _____ unto him the _____ _ that are _____ in this book."

BRIEF ANSWERS

1. Authority is _____

2. Name two things we must recognize concerning authority (See Lesson 1.).

    a. _____

    b. _____

3. Define "iniquity." _____

4. How do the New King James Version and New American Standard Bible read in Matthew 7:23? _____

5. What shall be done with them which do iniquity? _____

6. In whose name must all things be done? _____

7. What is the condition of entering into the kingdom of heaven? ____

8. If one transgresses the doctrine of Christ, what is his condition before God? _____

9. What makes one wise in God's sight? _____

10. God forbids our thinking of men above what? _____

TALK TIME — DISCUSSION

1. Study Matthew 7:21-23.

    a. Tell who can and who cannot enter into the kingdom. _____
    _____

    b. Will there be some good religious people turned away? _____

    c. Why will the Lord say unto some, "Depart from me"? _____
    _____

2. Read Matthew 7:24-29.

    a. What made the wise man wise? _____
    and the foolish man foolish? _____

LESSON 4 Authority – Our Need of It as Seen in the New Testament (Questions)

    b. In the spiritual realm who is the wise man? _____
Who is the foolish man? _____

    c. Does this paragraph relate to the need of authority? _____ And respecting authority? _____ If so, how? _____
_____

3. What does it mean to walk by the same rule (Phil. 3:16)? _____
_____

    a. What are some illustrations of walking by the same rule? _____
_____

    b. Can we be of the same mind if we do not recognize the same standard of authority? _____

4. Read 1 Corinthians 4:6. Be sure to compare the Revised Standard Version.

    a. What is the charge given to God's people in this reference? _____
_____

    b. Compare this verse to 2 John 9-11. Do they teach the same lesson? _____

5. What or who is condemned in Revelation 22:18-19? _____
_____

6. What does "in the name of the Lord Jesus" mean in Colossians 3:17?
_____

7. Read Matthew 21:23-27. Be prepared to answer the following questions:

    a. Do these Jews recognize a need for authority? _____

    b. Do they recognize that authority must come from one who has the right to give it? _____

    c. Does the answer of Jesus show His recognition of these things? _____

    d. The answer Jesus gives shows that there are only two sources of authority. What are they?

        i. _____

        ii. _____

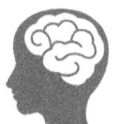

THINK! "THINK ON THESE THINGS"

1. Since those who work iniquity (practice lawlessness) will be rejected, is it safe to contend we do not need authority for all that we do? THINK!_____

   a. If you are not sure of your answer, then read Matthew 13:41-42.

2. The wise man is the man who hears the word of the Lord and obeys. Does this mean we should do all His Word IF it seems reasonable to us? THINK! _____

3. If we walk by the same rule, we will have unity. When division exists, what is apparent? THINK! _____
   Does it show we are not walking by the same rule? THINK! _____

4. Since transgressing the doctrine of Christ means one is without God and without Christ, should we do anything that is not authorized in the doctrine of Christ? THINK!_____

TRUE OR FALSE

1. Jesus says the man who does not build a house is foolish. _____
2. The Bible says all good, honest people will enter the kingdom of heaven. _____
3. The opinion of men is as dependable as the Word of God. _____
4. God can take one's name out of the book of life. _____
5. John says, if a man is sincerely teaching what he believes to be right, you should encourage him in every possible way (2 John 9-11). _____

WHAT YOU SHOULD LEARN FROM THIS LESSON

1. It is sinful to act without authority or to work iniquity.
2. Those who enter the kingdom must do the will of the Father in heaven.

LESSON 4 Authority – Our Need of It as Seen in the New Testament (Questions)

3. It is foolish to learn God's Word and refuse to obey it, but it is always wise to do the will of God.
4. God's people must walk by the same rule if unity is to prevail.
5. Going beyond that which is written is sinful.
6. We must do all things in the name of the Lord (by His authority).

Lesson 5

The Source of Authority

INTRODUCTION

1. Read Matthew 21:23-27, which focuses attention upon the importance of authority.
    a. The chief priests and elders had not authorized Christ to teach or to do what He had been doing, so they inquire about His authority and the source of it.
    b. They possibly think that they could destroy a great deal of His influence by showing that he taught and acted without authority from them.
2. Define authority (See introduction of Lesson No. 1.).
3. In previous lessons we showed the need for divine authority in the realm of religion. This need was illustrated from . . .
    a. Examples of the Old Testament—Cain and Abel, Nadab and Abihu, and Uzziah and the incense.
    b. The teaching of the New Testament—by Christ and by the Apostles.
4. In this lesson we shall be concerned with establishing the source of authority.
    a. The chief priests and elders who come to Christ ask, "and who gave thee this authority?"
    b. This shows the importance of the source of authority.
        i. Some things in religion are accepted as authoritative without consideration being given to the source from which they are derived.
        ii. We not only must have authority, we must have authority that comes from the right source.

I. The Source of Divine Authority Is Not . . .
    A. The doctrine or practices of the Old Testament.

1. Many fail to realize this and appeal to this part of God's Word as authority. Examples of this are in these religious practices:
   a. Tithing as the law of giving
   b. Instrumental music in worship
   c. Infant church membership
   d. Polygamy of the Mormons
2. They fail to recognize that the Old Testament system was only a shadow (Heb. 10:1) and was removed when Christ died on the cross (Eph. 2:14-16).

B. What the preachers say.
   1. Many regard the preacher's word as authority in religion.
      a. Perhaps this stems from the sectarian concept that the preacher has to be "called by the Lord" to preach.
      b. One of the most ridiculous spectacles of the religious realm is the diversity of doctrines that "God-called preachers" teach.
   2. Preachers are to preach the Word (2 Tim. 4:1-2), not "their" word.

C. Creeds of men.
   1. Practically every denomination has its manual, discipline, prayer book, or book of minutes that contains its doctrines and procedures for organizing a church of that kind.
      a. There was a time when these creeds were much more highly respected than they are today. At one time, rejection of the creed resulted in expulsion from that religious order.
   2. We cannot please God by accepting the creeds of men (Matt. 15:9; Col. 2:21-22).

D. Desires of the congregation.
   1. Some religious organizations take pride in the fact that they are democratic and that their policies are determined by majority vote.

2. The wishes of the congregation may not be right.
   a. Israel wanted gods to go before them (Ex. 32).
   b. Israel wanted a king (1 Sam. 8).
   c. King Saul says, "The people wanted to do this (1 Sam. 15:15, 24).
3. Desires of people are usually contrary to the wishes of the Lord.

E. Elders of a local church.
   1. Elders are to tend the flock (1 Pet. 5:2) and exercise the oversight of it (Acts 20:28) as shepherds, but they are under the authority of the chief Shepherd and have no legislative power in matters of faith.
   2. Some assume that the elders have such power.
      a. One gospel (?) preacher said he would have no objection to the use of instrumental music in worship if the elders authorized it.
      b. One brother told a woman she could stay home and iron her clothes on Sunday morning and worship Sunday night if the elders said it was alright.
   3. Elders are under the authority of Christ and have no legislative power. Hence, unauthorized practices and organizations cannot be made scriptural by being under their oversight (1 Pet. 5:1-4).

F. The results accomplished.
   1. Some assume that a thing being a good work or it accomplishing big results is sufficient authority for its existence. They assume that the end justifies the means.
   2. This fails to qualify a thing as a safe practice in religion.
      a. David gets results with the cart that bore the ark of the covenant, but it is not authorized as the way for moving the ark (2 Sam. 6:1-11; 1 Chron. 13:1-11).
      b. Uzziah is trying to engage in a good work when he wants to burn incense to the Lord, but it isn't a good work that God had authorized him to do (2 Chron. 26:16-20).

c. The fire Nadab and Abihu used to burn incense is getting results, but that does not make it right (Lev. 10:1-2).

CONCLUSION

1. We have established the need for authority, and that authority must come from the proper source.
2. In this lesson we show what the source of authority in religion IS NOT.

The Source of Authority (Questions)

 **WHAT DOES THE SCRIPTURE SAY?**

References: Matt. 21:23-27; Col. 2:14; Eph. 2:14-16; 2 Tim. 4:1-2; 1 Sam. 15:25; 1 Peter 5:1-2; Acts 20:28; 2 Sam. 6:1-11; Acts 15:1; Gal. 5:1-6

1. "By what _____ doest thou _____ _____ and who gave thee this _____?"

2. "And took _____ out of the _____, nailing it to the _____."

3. "For he is our _____, who hath made _____ one and hath _____ down the _____ wall of partition between us."

4. "For the _____ will come when _____ will not _____ _____ doctrine."

5. "Because I _____ the _____, _____ and their voice."

6. "Feed the _____ of God which is among you, taking the _____ thereof."

7. "To feed the _____ of God which he hath _____ with his own _____."

8. "Uzzah put forth his _____ to the _____ of God and took hold of it."

32 A Study of Authority

BRIEF ANSWERS

1. In previous lessons how did we illustrate the need for authority . . .

    a. From the Old Testament? _____

    b. From the New Testament? _____

2. How does Matthew 21:23-27 emphasize the source of authority?____
   _____

    a. Why are the chief priests and elders afraid to answer Jesus?
       _____

3. What passage shows that the Old Testament is not the source of authority? _____

TALK TIME — DISCUSSION

1. In apostolic days some tried to use the law of Moses as the source of authority (See Acts 15:1 and Gal. 5:1-6 regarding the matter of circumcision.).

    a. Why was this wrong (Read Eph. 2:12-14.)? _____

    b. Is it sinful to circumcise today? _____ If so, when?_____

2. Name some religious practices of today that are authorized or sought to be authorized by the Old Testament. _____
   _____

3. Read 1 Peter 5:1-4.

    a. How are elders to oversee? _____

    b. How does this passage show that elders are not the source of authority?_____

4. Read 2 Timothy 4:1-5.

    a. How does this show that the word of preachers is not the right source of authority? _____

LESSON 6 The Source of Authority (Questions)   33

    b. If we ask a man why he preaches a particular doctrine should he be able to tell us? _____

    c. Suppose he can only say, "I think," what then? _____

5. Knowing that human creeds are wrong in religion (See last lesson. Col. 2:20-22; Matt. 15:9), would it be safe for us to practice something just because men think it right? _____ Could we have an unwritten creed? _____

6. Read Exodus 32:1-6. What lesson regarding the desires of a congregation should we learn from this? _____

7. After reading 1 Samuel 1:8-9, be able to tell why the desires of Israel did not please God. _____

    a. Should we rely upon our desires as a source of authority? _____

8. Read 2 Samuel 6:1-11. Be prepared to explain why getting results is not the proper source of authority. _____

9. Read again Matthew 21:23-27.

    a. Tell the two sources of authority. _____

    b. Which source should we seek? _____

DO YOU KNOW YOUR BIBLE?

_____ Tithing was practiced   1. The Word

_____ From heaven   2. Lords over God's heritage

_____ Are made nigh   3. Unto yourselves

_____ Breaking down   4. Under the law of Moses

_____ Preach   5. This authority

_____ When they will not   6. The middle wall of partition

_____ After their own lusts   7. Or of men

_____ Who gave thee   8. By the blood of Christ

_____ Take heed therefore   9. Shall they heap to themselves

_____ Neither as being   10. Endure sound doctrine

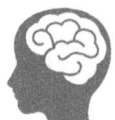 **THINK! "THINK ON THESE THINGS"**

1. Since the Lord called upon men for authority for their action should we know by whose authority we do what we do in religion? THINK! _____

2. Elders are to oversee, but not as lords. Then in what sense do they have authority? THINK! _____
What is the extent of their authority? THINK! _____
Are we to do anything the elders ask us to do? THINK! _____

3. Many people look to the preacher as a source of authority. Does he have a right to command men? THINK! _____ What should restrict his preaching? THINK! _____
Do all preachers respect this restriction? THINK! _____

4. Knowing that Israel sinned by doing that which the majority desired, should we do things just because the majority of the church wants to do it? THINK! _____ If so under what circumstances? THINK! _____
What does majority prove in religion? THINK! _____
What does it prove in the church? THINK! _____

5. If getting results did not authorize the action of David (2 Sam. 6) or of Nadab and Abihu (Lev. 10), should we conclude that it is sufficient authority for us? THINK! _____

6. If a practice of the church is called into question and we are unable to give Bible authority for it, should we stop it? THINK! _____

WHAT YOU SHOULD LEARN FROM THIS LESSON

1. There are two sources of authority—divine and human.
2. We cannot authorize a practice by appealing to the Old Testament.
3. It is wrong to listen to preachers or elders as sources of authority.
4. The church is not governed by the majority vote of its members.
5. The elders of the church do not have the right to make laws.
6. A program being big or successful (one that gets results) does not prove that it is right before God.

Lesson 7

The Source of Authority – What It Is

INTRODUCTION

1. We must have authority for all that we do (See Lessons 1 and 3.).
2. There are only two sources of authority—heaven and men.
3. In the last lesson we noted that the source of authority is not the Old Testament, preachers, creeds of men, desires of a congregation, elders, or results accomplished.
4. In this lesson we note the positive side of the source of authority.

I. Jesus Christ Is the Source of Authority
   A. He is God's ordained spokesman (Matt. 17:1-5; Heb. 1:1).
      1. God requires that we hear Him (Deut. 18:18-19; Acts 3:22-23).
   B. He has all authority in heaven and earth (Matt. 28:18).
      1. The Father in heaven, who has the rightful power, gave Him this and put all things under Him, with the exception of Himself (1 Cor. 15:27).
      2. He is "Lord of lords" (1 Tim. 6:15).
   C. He is the King raised up to sit on David's throne.
      1. God had promised David, "And thine house and thy kingdom shall be established for ever before thee: thy throne shall be established forever" (2 Sam. 7:16).
      2. Though the house of David had fallen down (Acts 15:16), God promised to set it up again.
         a. This he did in raising Christ to sit on David's throne (Acts 2:30-36).
      3. Christ is now King and will reign as such until His last enemy is destroyed (1 Cor. 15:24-26), then He will turn the kingdom back to God, the Father.
   D. He is the head of the body, the church (Eph. 1:22-23; Col. 1:18).

1. As members of the physical body are in subjection to the head, so must it be in the body of Christ.
   a. Christ is the head of the body; Christians are the members of the body.
2. The church is His bride; as the husband is the head of the wife and she is subject to him, so the church is to be in subjection to Christ (Eph. 5:23-24).
   a. Note: Verse 24 says, "so let the wives be to their own husbands in everything." A husband might demand of his wife that which would be contrary to the Lord's will, in which case she is to obey her Lord rather than her husband. BUT CHRIST WILL MAKE NO SUCH DEMANDS upon His bride; therefore, she is to be subject to Him in everything.

E. All things must be done in His name (Col. 3:17).
   1. "Whatsoever ye do in word" would include all teaching.
      a. No doctrine is to be taught unless authorized by the Lord (See 2 John 9-10.).
   2. "Whatsoever ye do in . . . deed" would include every work the people of God are to do.
      a. God's people are to do only the work that the Lord has authorized.
   3. Some are not content to be restricted by the will of Christ.
      a. They teach "for doctrines the commandments of men" (Matt. 15:9).
      b. They engage in works of iniquity (lawlessness) (Matt. 7:23).

   Note: The fact that "whatsoever [we] do in word or deed" must be done in the name of Christ shows the completeness of the authority of Christ.

CONCLUSION

1. We have defined authority and established man's need for it in religion.
2. We have illustrated that this authority must come from the right source.

3. We have established that Christ has the right to command; He has jurisdiction or legal authority as
    a. God's ordained spokesman.
    b. One who has all authority in heaven and earth.
    c. The seed of David reigning as King.
    d. The head of the body, the church.
    e. One in whose name all teaching and practice must be done.

Lesson 8

The Source of Authority – What It Is (Questions)

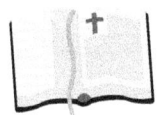

WHAT DOES THE SCRIPTURE SAY?

References: Matt. 17:1-5; Heb. 1:1, 2; Acts 3:22-23; Matt. 28:18; 1 Cor. 15:25-26; Col. 1:18; Acts 2:36; Col. 3:17

1. "This is _____ beloved _____, in whom _____ am _____ pleased; _____ ye _____."
2. "God who at sundry _____ and in _____ _____ manners spake in time _____ unto the _____ by the _____, hath in these _____ _____ spoken unto us by _____."
3. "And it shall come to pass that every _____ which will _____ _____ unto that _____, shall be from among the people."
4. "All _____ is given unto _____ in _____ and in _____."
5. "For he must _____ till he hath put all _____ under his _____. The last _____ that shall be destroyed is _____."
6. "And he is the _____ of the _____, the _____ . . . that in all things _____ might have the _____."
7. "Therefore let all the _____ of _____ know assuredly, that _____ hath made that same _____, whom ye crucified, both _____ and _____."
8. "And whatsoever ye do in _____ or _____, do all in the _____ of the Lord Jesus."

BRIEF ANSWERS

1. We have studied six things that are not the source of authority. Name them. _____
   _____

2. Of what was Jesus made to be head? _____
   What does this mean? _____

3. How does Matthew 28:18 read in the Revised Standard Version? What word is used instead of the word power? _____

4. What does "Lord" mean? _____

5. Where is Christ now sitting? _____

6. For whom did Peter, James, and John want to build tabernacles? _____
   _____

TALK TIME — DISCUSSION

1. Read Matthew 3:17 and Matthew 17:1-5. Be prepared to tell
   a. The relation of Jesus to the Father. _____
   b. The attitude of the Father toward Jesus. _____
   c. God's charge to us concerning Jesus. _____
   d. What, if anything, is significant about the appearance of Moses and Elias (Elijah)? Do they represent anything (Luke 16:16)? _____
   _____

2. After reading Hebrews 1:1-2, explain the difference in how God has spoken and how He now speaks. _____
   _____

3. Compare Deuteronomy 18:18-19 to Acts 3:22-23.
   a. How do they compare? _____
   b. Who is the prophet? _____

LESSON 8 The Source of Authority – What It Is (Questions)

4. How much authority does Jesus have (Matt. 28:18)? _____
   a. How much does Moses and the law have? _____
   b. Were the ten commandments a part of Moses' law? _____
   c. How much does David have? _____
5. Study the first gospel sermon (Acts 2:22-36). Be prepared to answer the following:
   a. Did Peter preach that Jesus was sitting on David's throne? _____
   b. How long will Jesus reign (See also 1 Cor. 15:25-26)? _____
   c. Does this mean He is now reigning? _____
   d. Is the King the right source of authority in the kingdom? _____
6. Read Ephesians 1:22-23 and Colossians 1:18 and be able to discuss the following:
   a. To what place did God exalt Jesus? _____
   b. When was He thus exalted? _____
   c. Is there a difference between the body and the church? _____
   d. Does the head of the body have authority over the body? _____
7. After reading Ephesians 5:23-24 be prepared to tell the following:
   a. The husband is the head of the wife, as what? _____
      _____
   b. To whom should the church be in subjection? _____
   c. Will Christ make demands of the church that are impossible for the church to meet? _____
8. Read Colossians 3:17.
   a. What does "in the name of" mean in this passage? _____
   b. Discuss the expression "in word or deed." What does this include?
      _____

TRUE OR FALSE

1. Moses and the prophets have some authority, but not as much as Jesus. _____
2. Jesus is of the house of David. _____
3. Christ destroyed the last enemy when He ascended to heaven. _____
4. Jesus will sit upon the throne of David in the city of Jerusalem. _____
5. The Bible says the church is subject to Christ. _____
6. Christ is the head of the church even as the husband is the head of the wife. _____

THINK! "THINK ON THESE THINGS"

1. Jesus has all authority in heaven and earth. Who gave Him this authority? THINK! _____ What about conferences, councils, and boards of men? Do they have authority in religion? THINK! _____ Who gave them this authority? THINK! _____
2. Of Jesus, God says, "Hear ye him." What is involved in hearing Jesus? Does He speak to us in a dream? In a still small voice? If not, how can we hear Him? THINK! _____
3. How does being head of the body give Christ authority over it? THINK! _____
4. Whatsoever we do in word or deed is to be done in the name of the Lord Jesus. How does this show the authority of Christ? THINK! _____

WHAT YOU SHOULD LEARN FROM THIS LESSON

1. Jesus Christ is the only true source of authority today. If we please God we must hear Him. We are not permitted to do anything without His authority if we want the favor of God.

The Authority of Jesus Christ Is Set Forth in the New Testament

INTRODUCTION

1. In preceding lessons we have showed the need for authority in religion and that there are only two sources or authority—divine and human.
2. We have studied the source of authority from both the negative and the positive viewpoint, emphasizing that Jesus is the source of authority today.
3. In this lesson we show that the authority of Christ is set forth in the New Testament.
   a. We have not seen Jesus.
   b. Jesus does not speak to us directly.

I. The New Testament Is the Will of Jesus
   A. God had promised to make a "NEW COVENANT" (Jer. 31:31-34).
      1. This promise and subsequent giving of the new covenant is what made the "first covenant" the "old" covenant (Heb. 8:13).
         a. When God established the first covenant (Ex. 19-20) it was not "old."
         b. It was made "old" by the giving of a new covenant.
   B. The New Testament is the "new covenant," the will of Jesus.
      1. He is the mediator of the New Testament (Heb. 9:14-17; 8:6-13).
      2. The blood of Jesus dedicated the New Testament (Matt. 26:28).
      3. It was not preached until after the death of Jesus (cf. Heb. 9:16-17).
   C. The first covenant (old law) was abolished that the new covenant might be inaugurated.

1. Jesus came to fulfill the law and the prophets (Matt. 5:17).
2. In His death on the cross He took away the old covenant that His will, the New Testament, might begin to be preached unto men (Heb. 10:9-10).
   a. The old covenant is "the middle wall of partition" that separated the Jews from the Gentiles. Jesus has broken down this wall of partition (Eph. 2:14-17).
   b. The old covenant was a "schoolmaster to bring" the Jews to Christ, but "we are no longer under a schoolmaster" (Gal. 3:24-25).

II. The New Testament Is God's Message Unto Men in This Dispensation
   A. God speaks to us by His Son (Heb. 1:1).
      1. God has spoken by the prophets. This was true in old testament days.
      2. God now speaks by His Son.
         a. His message through His Son is the New Testament.
   B. Jesus spoke through the apostles who were his witnesses and ambassadors (Luke 24:46-48; Acts 1:8; 2 Cor. 5:20).
      1. Apostles were eye witnesses (Cf. Acts 1:21-22; 2 Pet. 1:16).
         a. This is why the Lord appeared unto Saul of Tarsus (Acts 26:16).
         b. Thus, Paul speaks of himself as "one born out of due time" (1 Cor. 15:8).
      2. Apostles were chosen ambassadors (2 Cor. 5:18).
         a. An ambassador is one sent forth as an official representative.
      3. When the apostles spoke, they represented Christ, and their word must be received as the word of Christ (Matt. 10:40; Luke 10:16; John 13:20).
         a. The Holy Spirit guided them; thus, they never preached error (cf. John 16:13; Gal. 1:11-12).
         b. Those who received the apostles received Christ; those who rejected the apostles rejected Christ who sent them.

LESSON 9 The Authority of Jesus Christ Is Set Forth in the New Testament

    C. The apostles and other inspired men wrote the truth that was revealed unto them. Their writings are known as the New Testament.

        1. Some facts regarding their writings (the New Testament)

            a. It is a divine message, the Word of God (1 Thess. 2:13).

            b. It is a complete message (John 15:13; 2 Tim. 3:16-17).

            c. It is the final message (Jude 3—"Once delivered unto the saints." cf. Heb. 9:28).

CONCLUSION

1. Jesus is the source of authority today. But He is not speaking directly unto every soul; He is speaking through the words of the New Testament. Therefore, the will of Christ is set forth in the New Testament.

2. Hence, everything we teach or practice must be authorized in the New Testament.

The Authority of Jesus Christ Is Set Forth in the New Testament (Questions)

Lesson 10

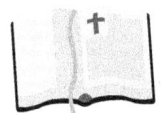 **WHAT DOES THE SCRIPTURE SAY?**

References: Jer. 31:31-34; Heb. 8:13; Heb. 9:15-17; Heb. 10:9; Gal. 3:24-25; Heb. 1:1; Acts 1:8; 2 Cor. 5:20; Matt. 10:40; 1 Thess. 2:13

1. "Behold, the days come, saith the _____ , that I will make a _____ _____ with the house of _____ , and with the house of Judah."

2. "In that he said, a _____ covenant, he hath made the first _____ ."

3. "And for this cause he is the _____ of the new testament, that by means of _____ , for the redemption of the transgressions that were under the _____ testament, they which are called might receive the promise of eternal inheritance."

4. "For where a _____ is, there must also of necessity be the _____ of the testator."

5. "He taketh away the _____ , that he may establish the _____ ."

6. "Wherefore the law was our _____ to bring us unto Christ, that we might be justified by _____ . But after that faith is come, we are no longer under a schoolmaster."

7. "God, who at sundry times and in diverse manners spake in _____ _____ _____ unto the fathers by the prophets, hath in these _____ days spoken unto us by his _____ ."

8. "But ye shall receive _____ , after the Holy Spirit is come upon you: and ye shall be _____ unto me both in Jerusalem, and in all Judea, and in Samaria, and unto the _____ part of the earth."

9. "Now then we are _____ for Christ, as though God did beseech you by us: We pray you in Christ's stead, be ye _____ to God."

10. "He that receiveth you _____ me, and he that receiveth me _____ him that sent me."

11. "For this cause also thank we God without ceasing, because when ye receive the word of God which ye heard _____ _____, ye received it not as the word of _____, but as it is in truth, the word of _____ which effectually worketh also in you that believe."

BRIEF ANSWERS

1. What did God promise to make in the last days with the house of Israel and the house of Judah? _____

2. What is a covenant? _____

3. What is necessary before a testament is of force? _____

4. Since the first testament was in effect when Jesus came to this world, what had to be done with the first testament before a second one could be given? _____

5. Who were the witnesses and ambassadors of Christ? _____

6. How can we know that the apostles made no errors in their preaching? _____

TALK TIME — DISCUSSION

1. Read Jeremiah 31:31-34 and Hebrews 8:7-13. What are some provisions that would be made in this "new covenant?" _____

LESSON 10 The Authority of Jesus Christ Is Set Forth in the New Testament
(Questions)

2. The apostles were "witnesses" of Christ (Lk. 24:46-48; Acts 1:8).

   a. What does the word witness imply? _____

   b. Was being an eyewitness of Christ after His resurrection a condition of being an apostle? (See Acts 1:21-23.) _____

   c. Why did the Lord appear unto Saul of Tarsus? (See Acts 26:16.)
   _____

   d. Can we be "witnesses" for Christ today? _____ If not, why not?
   _____

3. What does "ambassador" mean? _____

   a. Who were the chosen ambassadors of Christ (2 Cor. 5:20)? _____
   _____

   b. Are we His ambassadors today? _____

   c. Be prepared to discuss how we are to receive the words of these ambassadors (See Matt. 10:40; Luke 10:16; John 13:20.). _____
   _____

4. For what purpose was the Holy Spirit sent unto the apostles (John 16:13)? _____
   _____

   a. Did the Spirit guide the apostles into all truth? _____

5. List four facts regarding the writings of the apostles and other inspired men of their generation.

   a. _____
   b. _____
   c. _____
   d. _____

6. Read 2 Timothy 3:16-17. List four things for which the Scripture is profitable.

   a. _____   b. _____
   c. _____   d. _____

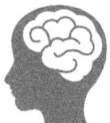 **THINK! "THINK ON THESE THINGS"**

1. God made a covenant (first covenant) with the Israelites. Why did He want to make a new covenant? THINK! _____
   _____

2. Paul says, "the law was our schoolmaster to bring us unto Christ, that we might be justified by faith. But after that faith is come, we are no longer under a schoolmaster." What does this mean? THINK! _____
   _____

3. God has spoken unto the fathers by the prophets, but now speaks by His Son (Heb. 1:1-2). Does this mean the prophets have the same authority as the Son of God? THINK! _____

4. Jesus says to the apostles, "he that heareth you heareth me; and he that despiseth you despiseth me; and he that despiseth me despiseth him that sent me." If we do not hear the words of the apostles, what is our attitude toward God and Christ? THINK! _____

5. Hebrews 1:1-2 declares that God now speaks by His Son.
   a. Have you ever heard the voice of Jesus? _____ Has he talked to you? _____
   b. Have you ever seen Jesus Christ? _____
   c. Then how does God speak unto us by His Son? THINK! _____
      _____

6. Jude says the faith "was once delivered unto the saints" (Jude 3). The writer of Hebrews says, "Christ was once offered to bear the sins of many" (Heb. 9:28). If Christ being "once offered" means He will never be offered again, then what does it mean when Jude says the faith was "once delivered"? THINK! _____
   _____

   Is God still delivering His word to chosen men? THINK! _____

LESSON 10 The Authority of Jesus Christ Is Set Forth in the New Testament
(Questions)

 **WHAT YOU SHOULD LEARN FROM THIS LESSON**

1. God now, in these last days, speaks unto us by His Son.
2. Jesus speaks unto us through His chosen ambassadors, the apostles.
3. The apostles and other inspired men of their generation wrote the words of the Lord in twenty seven books (letters or epistles) which are known as the New Testament.
4. The will of Jesus Christ is set forth in the New Testament.
5. Everything we teach or practice must be authorized in the New Testament, or it cannot be done by the authority of Christ.

How to Establish Authority

INTRODUCTION

1. In past lessons we have learned
   a. What authority is and our need for it in religion.
   b. That the source of authority today is not the Old Testament, the preacher's word, creeds of men, desires of a congregation, the elders of a local church, or the fact that a thing gets results.
   c. That Christ is the right source of authority because He is God's spokesman; He has all authority in heaven and earth; He is the king and head of the church.
   d. That the will of Christ is set forth in the New Testament.
2. As we pursue the study of authority, we are interested in learning how God teaches us or how to establish authority.

I. How to Establish Authority

   A. God teaches us in one of three ways:

   1. "May I suggest to you now that there are three ways by which God teaches us his will, his word, his way. Now hear them: First, he teaches by direct statement, by positive command, saying the thing in so many words. Now that is one way. Well, there is another. You might not have a direct "Thus saith the Lord," but if you can find an example approved and inspired of God, that concrete example comes to us with all the power and force of divine authority. That is God's way of teaching. Then again, if there is a passage in the Bible from which a necessary conclusion and inference must be drawn, I am willing to accept the statement that the Bible teaches that thing. So watch them. How does God teach us? First, by direct statement. Second, by approved example. Third, by a necessary inference." (N.B. Hardeman, *Hardeman's Tabernacle Sermons*, Vol. IV, page 52, 1938 edition).

2. Note: We do not quote brother Hardeman as a source of authority, but rather to show that brethren have long recognized that there are but three ways of establishing authority.
B. The three ways by which authority may be established.
   1. Direct statement or command
      a. Examples:
         i. All must repent (Acts 17:30; Luke 13:3).
         ii. Disciples are to contribute (1 Cor. 16:1-2).
         iii. The assembling of saints (Heb. 10:25)
         iv. It is wrong to lie (Col. 3:9).
   2. Approved example (example approved by an inspired man)
      a. Examples:
         i. Breaking bread on the first day of the week (Acts 20:7)
         ii. Churches sending to the relief of others in benevolence (Acts 11:29-30)
   3. Necessary inference
      a. An inference is a logical conclusion drawn from given data or premises. A necessary inference is a conclusion that is necessary.
      b. Examples of necessary inference
         i. Lot went down into Egypt with Abram (Gen. 13:1; 12:10).
         ii. Before He was baptized, Jesus went down into the water (Matt. 3:16).
C. These three ways of establishing authority illustrated by the Lord's Supper
   1. We learn **what** to eat and drink by a DIRECT STATEMENT (Matt. 26:26-28).
      a. "Jesus took bread . . . he took the cup" (Note: We know the cup is "the fruit of the vine," cf. Luke 22:18.).

b. This is why we still use the bread and fruit of the vine.
 2. We know **when** to eat and drink by APPROVED EXAMPLE (Acts 20:7).
    a. This is the only reference to the day on which the disciples met to break bread.
    b. To break bread on any other day would be to act without authority from the Lord.
 3. We know the **frequency** of eating by a NECESSARY INFERENCE (Acts 20:7).
    a. Since the disciples met upon the first day of the week, it is necessarily inferred that it was a weekly occurrence.
       i. When a thing is to be observed only one time a year, the month and the day of the month must be specified.
          a. Your birthday
          b. Pentecost day—the morrow after the seventh sabbath from the sabbath of the Passover (Lev. 23:15-16), thus, always fifty days from the sabbath of the Passover
       ii. Things to be observed one time each month must be specified by the day of the month.
          a. Rent, a payment, or one's salary may be received on the first day of the month, or any particular day.
       iii. For a weekly observance, only the day of the week needs to be specified.
          a. "The seventh day is the sabbath of the Lord thy God" (Ex. 20:10). He did not say "every seventh day," but it was necessarily inferred, and the Jews understood.

II. Putting What We Have Learned Into Practice
 A. By using the three ways of establishing authority, you should be able to determine whether the following things are authorized or unauthorized.

1. The kingdom was established on Pentecost day (cf. Mark 9:1; Acts 1:4-8; 2:1-4). Which of the three ways are used to establish this truth?
2. Baptism to the penitent believer is for the remission of sins (Acts 2:38). Which of the three ways were used?
3. What about counting of beads? Burning incense? Offering animal sacrifices? Confessing sins to a priest? Sprinkling for baptism? Thursday night communion?

CONCLUSION

1. Authority must come from the Lord.
2. Authority may be established by a direct statement, approved apostolic example, or a necessary inference.
3. If there is no direct statement, no approved example, or no necessary inference, then it is not authorized and is, therefore, sinful.

Lesson 12

How to Establish Authority (Questions)

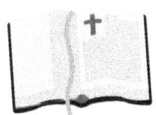 **WHAT DOES THE SCRIPTURE SAY?**

References: Acts 17:30; 1 Cor. 16:1-2; Heb. 10:25; Col. 3:9; Acts 20:7; Matt. 3:16; Acts 2:38; Matt. 26:26-28; 1 Cor. 6:12; 1 Cor. 10:23; Ex. 20:10

1. "And the times of this _____ God _____ at; but now commandeth all men _____ to _____."

2. "_____ the _____ day of the _____ let every _____ of you _____ by him in _____ as God hath _____."

3. "Not _____ the _____ of ourselves together, as the manner of some is."

4. "And _____ the _____ _____ of the _____ when the _____ came together to _____ bread."

5. "And _____ when he was _____ went up _____ out of the water."

6. "_____ and be _____ every one of you in the _____ of _____ Christ for the _____ of sins."

7. "Jesus took _____, and blessed it, and _____ it, and gave _____ to the _____, and said, _____ _____; this is my _____."

8. "And he _____ the _____ and gave _____, and gave it to the _____ saying, _____ ye _____ of it."

9. "All things are _____ unto me, but _____ things are not _____."

10. "But the _____ day is the _____ of the _____ thy God."

BRIEF ANSWERS

1. How do you know that authority is needed in religion? _____
   _____

2. Who is the right source of authority? _____

3. Who is quoted in this lesson, and why is he quoted? _____
   _____

4. What are the three ways of establishing authority? _____
   _____

TALK TIME — DISCUSSION

1. Be prepared to discuss the direct statement or command as a way of establishing authority. _____
   _____

   a. Read Luke 13:3. What does this authorize us to teach? _____
      _____
      By what means? _____

   b. How does 1 Corinthians 16:1-2 illustrate the direct statement?
      _____

   c. After reading Hebrews 10:25 be able to tell what you learn from this verse, and how you know that. _____
      _____

   d. Does Colossians 3:9 illustrate the direct statement? _____

LESSON 12 How to Establish Authority (Questions)

2. Prepare yourself to talk about an approved example.
   a. What does it mean? _____
   _____
   b. What is the difference between this and a direct statement? ____
   _____
   c. Give an illustration of something learned by an approved example. _____
   _____

3. What is a necessary inference? _____
   _____
   a. Tell the difference between an inference and a necessary inference. _____
   _____
   b. Be ready to tell something you have learned by a necessary inference. _____
   _____

4. Show how the Lord's Supper illustrates the three ways of establishing authority. _____
   _____
   a. What is taught by commandment? _____
   b. What is taught by a necessary inference? _____
   c. What is taught by an approved example? _____

5. Why is it wrong to appeal to expediency as a means of establishing authority? _____
   _____

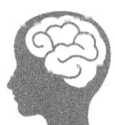 **THINK! "THINK ON THESE THINGS"**

1. From the example in Acts 20:7 we learn when to break bread, "upon the first day of the week." Since they are meeting in the "third loft" (v. 9),

why do we not follow that example? To help you answer this question read John 4:24. How must we worship God? THINK! _____

_____

2. Since there is only one example of meeting to break bread, how do we know this should be done every week? THINK! _____

_____

3. A principle is "a fundamental truth; a primary basic law, doctrine or the like; a settle rule of action; a governing law of conduct" (Webster). Can we have a principle without a statement, example, or necessary inference to establish it? THINK!_____

4. What is an expedient? THINK! _____

_____

TRUE OR FALSE

1. It is necessarily inferred that all men must repent. _____
2. Jesus commanded the disciples to eat the bread and drink the cup. _____
3. Jesus commanded the disciples to break bread on the first day of the week. _____
4. By a necessary inference we learn to break bread on the first day of the week. _____
5. For every principle there is a command, example, or necessary inference to establish it. _____
6. A thing must be expedient before it can be lawful. _____

WHAT YOU SHOULD LEARN FROM THIS LESSON

1. How to establish authority—the three means of establishing authority
2. That not all things are taught by a commandment

LESSON 12 How to Establish Authority (Questions)

3. An approved example is just as authoritative as a commandment.
4. The difference between an inference and a necessary inference and that only a necessary inference can establish a fact
5. How to apply the principles learned in this lesson and thus establish authority for all things we teach and practice
6. That in the absence of a direct command or an approved example or a necessary inference there is no authority from the Lord
7. It is always in order to call upon any teacher to show authority for what he is teaching.

How to Establish Authority (Application)

Lesson 13

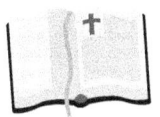

REVIEW

1. In past lessons we have learned that authority is needed for everything we teach or practice and that Jesus Christ is the source of authority.
2. In the last lesson we learned that authority is established in one of three ways: (1) Direct statement, (2) Approved example and (3) Necessary inference.
3. Give an illustration of
   a. Direct statement _____
   _____
   b. Approved example _____
   _____
   c. Necessary inference _____
   _____
4. We have learned that an approved example is as authoritative as a command.
5. We have learned that while many things may be inferred, only a necessary inference establishes a fact.

APPLYING WHAT WE HAVE LEARNED

Draw a line from the subject on the left to the circle on the right which you think will authorize the subject. On the line write the Scripture reference which establishes your point.

TEACHING/PRACTICE	THE AUTHORITY
_____ Faith in Christ	
_____ Repentance	
_____ Confession of faith	Direct Statement
_____ Baptism for remission of sins	
_____ Breaking of bread	
_____ Drinking the cup	
_____ Cup is the "fruit of the vine"	
_____ Unleavened bread	Approved Example
_____ Elders of the church	
_____ Weekly observance of Lord's supper	
_____ Assembling	
_____ Laying by . . . in store	
_____ Prayers	
_____ Singing	Necessary Inference
_____ Preaching the word	
_____ Church caring for its needy	
_____ Church supporting a preacher	
_____ Church having a place to meet	

Scriptures: Mark 16:16; Acts 20:7; Luke 13:3; 2 Tim. 4:2; Acts 4:34, 35; Matt. 10:32; Acts 2:38; Phil. 1:15; Matt. 26:26-28; Eph. 5:19; Acts 2:27; Matt. 26:17, 26; Acts 20:28; Heb. 10:25; 1 Cor. 16:1-2

LESSON 13 How to Establish Authority (Application)   65

 **APPLYING WHAT WE HAVE LEARNED (PART 2)**

This is part two of applying what we have learned. Draw a line from the subject in the column on the left to the circle in the column on the right that would authorize it. We have added one more circle on the right for this part of the exercise.

TEACHING/PRACTICE   **THE AUTHORITY**

_____ Sprinkling for baptism

_____ Burning incense   (Direct Statement)

_____ Sprinkling of holy water

_____ Counting of beads

_____ Bowing before images

_____ Baptizing of babies   (Approved Example)

_____ Instrumental music in worship

_____ Elders over two or more churches

_____ Women preachers

_____ Cake and coffee on the Lord's table   (Necessary Inference)

_____ Confessing sins to a priest

_____ Preachers called "Reverend"

_____ Majority rule in the church

_____ Church sponsored recreation   (Authorized ONLY BY MEN)

_____ Chicken dinners, ice cream socials

_____ Mourner's bench

_____ Church contributing to a missionary society

This should help you to understand why we do not teach or practice the subjects in the column on the left. We learned in a preceding lesson that all things are authorized either by heaven or by men (See Matt. 21:24.). Since Jesus has all authority (Matt. 28:18), this leaves no authority for men in the realm of religion. Therefore, we should reject that which only the authority of men teaches or practices.

 **QUESTION TIME**

Perhaps you have a question concerning some teaching or practice. We stand ready to give the New Testament authority for everything we teach or practice by referring either to a direct statement, an approved example, or a necessary inference. Write down any question to which you may want an answer, and bring it up during the class session._____
_____
_____

Lesson 14

Authority – Generic and Specific (Questions)

In previous lessons we have defined authority and showed our need for it. We have discussed improper sources of authority in religion and showed that Jesus Christ is the source of authority today. We have illustrated how we establish what Christ has authorized, i.e., by direct statement, approved example, or necessary inference.

There are two kinds of authority: generic and specific.

1. Generic means "general, opposite to specific" (Webster). Generic authority includes all the methods or ways for doing the thing authorized.

2. Specific means "precisely formulated or restricted; specifying or explicit" (Webster). Thus, specific authority restricts one to that which is precisely formulated or specified.

3. In this lesson we shall illustrate these two kinds of authority.

 **WHAT DOES THE SCRIPTURE SAY?**

References: Ex. 12:1-10; Gen. 6:14-16; Matt. 28:18-20; 26:26-28; Eph. 5:19; Col. 3:16; Luke 22:18

1. "Your lamb shall be _____, a _____ of the _____ year: ye shall take it out from the ___ ___ or from the _____."

2. "Make thee an _____ of _____ wood; rooms shalt thou make in the _____ and shalt _____ it within and without with _____."

3. "___ ___ ye therefore, and _____ all nations, _____ them in the _____ of the _____ and of the _____ and of the _____ _____."

4. "And as they were eating, Jesus took _____, and blessed it, and _____ it, and gave it to the disciples, and said, _____ _____ this is my _____. And he took the _____, and gave thanks, and gave it to them saying _____ ye all of it."

5. "Speaking to _____ in _____ and spiritual _____, _____ and making _____ in your heart to the Lord."

6. "Teaching and admonishing one another in _____ and hymns and spiritual _____ singing with _____ in your _____ to the Lord."

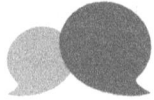 **BRIEF ANSWERS**

1. Define "generic." _____
   _____

2. Define "specific." _____
   _____

3. Authority may be established in one of three ways. Name them. _____
   _____

4. In Matthew's account of the great commission (Matt. 28:18-20) what four things did Jesus charge them to do? Note: We learn this by direct statement. _____
   _____

5. Did God specify the kind of wood which was to be used in building the ark? _____

TALK TIME — DISCUSSION

1. Whether a thing is authorized in a generic or specific sense will be learned by a direct statement, approved example, or necessary inference. Read Genesis 6:14. Subject: Making the ark.

LESSON 14 Authority – Generic and Specific (Questions)

   a. What material did God authorize? _____
      (Note: Wood is generic. Gopher wood is specific.)
   b. Name some other kinds of wood. _____
   c. Did God tell Noah not to use any other kind of wood? _____
   d. Why did he use gopher wood? _____

2. Read Exodus 12:5. Subject: Kind of sacrifice.
   a. Animal is a generic term.
   b. What does God specify? _____
   c. Name other specifics of this generic. _____
   d. Show how the command restricted the kind of animal to be offered. _____ _____
   _____
      i. Consider these terms: lamb, without blemish, male, first year, from sheep or goats. Does each term restrict the sacrifice to be offered? _____
      ii. Does each specific include some animals and exclude others?
   e. Was it necessary for God to name all the animals that are excluded? _____
   f. This illustrates specific authority. How? _____
   _____

3. Read Matthew 28:18-20. Subject: The great commission.
   a. The first command of this commission is GO.
      i. Is this generic or specific? _____
      ii. What are some specific ways of going? _____
      _____
      iii. What ways of going are authorized? _____
      _____
      iv. If it is not specifically mentioned, can it still be authorized? _____

v. When not specifically mentioned, must the general realm be authorized? _____

b. The second command of this commission is TEACH.

  i. Is this generic or specific? _____

  ii. What are specific ways of teaching? _____

  iii. How many methods of teaching are authorized? _____ How do you know? _____

c. To learn WHAT to teach read Mark 16:15-16.

  i. Does the Lord specify what to teach? _____ What is it? _____

  ii. Does this exclude other things? _____ How do you know? _____

4. Read Matthew 26:26-28. Subject: The Lord's Supper.

  a. Are the terms "eat" and "drink" generic or specific? _____ Explain your answer. _____

  b. Does the Lord specify what the disciples were to eat and drink? If so, what is specified? _____

  c. If the Lord gives no specific food or liquid which the disciples were to eat and drink, but merely commanded them to "eat" and "drink," what would have been authorized? _____

  d. When the Lord specifies "bread" and "fruit of the vine" (See Luke 22:18.), did this make all other foods and liquids unauthorized? ___

    i. Why not have cake and coffee? _____

    ii. Why not have cornbread and buttermilk? _____

    iii. Does the Lord say not to have these things? _____

LESSON 14 Authority – Generic and Specific (Questions)

    e. A specific authorizes that which is specified and makes all other specifics in that general realm unauthorized. Thus, by specifying "bread" and "fruit of the vine" the Lord authorized these, and all other foods and drinks are unauthorized (Note: Be sure that each student understands this principle.).

    f. There are many kinds of bread. Why do we use unleavened bread? _____

        i. Why not have hot rolls or French bread? _____

        ii. Did the Lord say not to use those (Read Matt. 26:17.)? _____

        iii. Do we know what the Lord used? _____

5. Read Ephesians 5:19. Subject: Kind of music in worship.

    a. Singing is a specific kind of music. Do you agree? _____

    b. What other kind of music is there? _____

    c. Does God say not to use the other kind? _____

    d. When the Lord specifies the kind to use, does this exclude the other kind and make it unauthorized? _____ Remember the lamb? The gopher wood? The unleavened bread? These are specifics that exclude everything else, for they are unauthorized.

    e. What kind of music is authorized in this passage? _____

    f. Before any other kind can be used, there must be authority for it. Right? _____

    g. What kind of songs are authorized? _____

        i. Is this specific? _____

        ii. Does this exclude, or make unauthorized, some good songs? _____

        Give an example. _____

WHAT YOU SHOULD LEARN FROM THIS LESSON

1. Generic authority authorizes everything in that general realm—all of the specifics in that realm. Thus, a thing **does not have to be mentioned in the scripture to be authorized**.

2. Specific authority authorizes that which is specified and excludes all other specifics in the general realm, for they are unauthorized. Thus, a thing **does not have to be specifically forbidden to be unauthorized**.

3. Learn these lessons well, for they are the cause of much confusion in religion.

Lesson 15

Expediency

INTRODUCTION

1. Men have sought to justify a multitude of things by saying, "They can be practiced as expediencies."
   a. The common concept: The end justifies the means, so anything that will accomplish what we think to be good, whether authorized or not, is permissible.
      i. Note: We have learned in a previous lesson that results accomplished does not authorize anything.
2. In order for a thing to be a scriptural expedient, it must facilitate in the accomplishment of God's will and must be in harmony with His Word.
3. Expediency in human wisdom involves the right of a choice within the realm of those things included in what God has authorized.

I. For a Thing to Be Expedient, It Must Be Lawful
   A. All scriptural expedients are lawful (1 Cor. 6:12; 10:23).
      1. They come within the realm of things authorized.
         a. Authority may be established by a direct statement, approved example, or a necessary inference.
      2. That which is not authorized is unlawful—prohibited by divine authority; thus, it is sinful (2 John 9-11).
         a. This involves going beyond that which is written (2 John 9-11).
         b. Going beyond the realm of faith (2 Cor. 5:7; Rom. 14:23).
      3. We have no assurance that a thing is pleasing unto God unless it is authorized in the Scripture.
         a. Thus, an expedient must first be lawful.

II. For a Thing to Be Expedient, It Cannot Be Specified
   A. When God specifies, there is no choice for man but to obey or disobey.

1. In matters specified, faith demands obedience to the Lord. Examples:
   a. God specifies gopher wood for the ark (Gen. 6:14). By faith Noah did all that God commanded (v. 22; cf. Heb. 11:7).
   b. God specifies a male lamb of the first year, without blemish, as a sacrifice (Ex. 12:5). The Israelites choose to obey.
2. Expediency in human wisdom involves the right of choice within the realm of those things included in what God has authorized.
   a. Noah could choose which gopher wood to use, whether a large or small log, etc., but he must use gopher wood to obey God.
   b. The Israelites could choose which male lamb, of the first year that was without blemish, should be offered, but they must offer such an animal in order to obey God.

B. To go beyond that which is specified or authorized is to add to God's word, not to aid obedience.
   1. God commands singing (Eph. 5:19; Col. 3:16).
      a. Instrumental music is not an aid in singing but is an addition to God's commandment.
   2. God commands to dip, submerge, bury in baptism (Rom. 6:4).
      a. Since God does not specify the place to baptize, a baptistery may expedite the accomplishment of God's will; thus, a baptistery is an expedient.
      b. Sprinkling for baptism is not expedient, for it is not lawful. It does not aid the accomplishment of God's will. It is a substitution for that which God commands, thus unlawful and sinful.
   3. God specifies that the oversight and function of elders be restricted to the local church (Acts 14:23; 20:28; 1 Pet. 5:1-4).
      a. For the elders of one church to oversee the members, monies or work of another church is not a matter of

expediency. Such is not lawful. It does not come within the realm of that which the Lord has authorized elders to work; thus, it is unlawful and sinful.

4. The local church is the organization God authorizes for preaching the gospel (1 Tim. 3:15; Eph. 4:12). While the church is not an organization, it has organization, and the only organization of the church is the local church (Acts 14:23; Phil. 1:1).

   a. A Missionary Society is not an aid, for it is not within the scope of that which is authorized.

   b. The Missionary Society is an addition to the organization which God authorizes. It is an organization which men have built to do the work God gives the church to do. It is unlawful and sinful.

III. For a Thing to Be Expedient It Must Edify (1 Cor. 10:23-33)

   A. All things are to "be done unto" edification (1 Cor. 14:26).

      1. If a thing be a matter of choice or expediency, falling into the realm of human wisdom or judgment, and its practice causes division in the body of Christ, it is sinful and wrong.

      2. When God commands, it must be done in spite of consequences, even if it divides people. If doing the will of God requires it, men have no choice but to obey.

         a. Example: preaching the word (Acts 4:18-20; 5:29)

      3. But if it is a non-essential—God having left the choice to human wisdom—and we demand or enforce that which destroys the unity and peace of God's children, we sin.

IV. For a Thing to Be Expedient It Must Not Offend the Conscience of a Brother (1 Cor. 10:32; Rom. 14:13-23)

   A. This rule governs only in matters of expediency.

      1. In matters specified we have no choice but to obey or disobey.

      2. Where the liberty of a choice by human wisdom has been permitted by the divine will, we must not force "our way" to the offending of a brother by causing him to violate his conscience in partaking in that which he believes to be wrong.

a. Example: eating of meat (1 Cor. 8:7-13)

V. An Addition to God's Word or a Substitution for God's Way Cannot Be Claimed as an Expedient

    A. An expedient must first be lawful.

        1. Every addition or substitution is unlawful. It is relying upon human wisdom.

        2. Such is not a matter of expediency but is a transgression of God's will.

CONCLUSION

1. Remember: Expediency involves the right of choice within the realm of that which is authorized in the New Testament and is not a course of authority within itself.

(Note: Much of the material in this lesson has been taken from *Walking by Faith*, by Roy Cogdill, pages 19-21, and you can purchase from One Stone Biblical Resources, 979 Lovers Lane, Bowling Green, Kentucky, 42103.)

Lesson 16

Expediency (Questions)

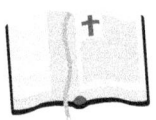 **WHAT DOES THE SCRIPTURE SAY?**

References: 1 Cor. 6:12; 2 Cor. 5:7; Rom. 14:23; 1 Cor. 10:23; Heb. 11:7; 1 Cor. 14:26; 1 Cor. 10:32; 8:7-13; Romans 14:20

1. "All things are _____ unto me, but _____ _____ are not _____: all things are _____ for me, but _____ _____ not be brought under the power of any."

2. "For we _____ by _____, not by _____."

3. "For whatsoever is not of _____ is _____."

4. "All things _____ _____ for me, but all things are not _____ all _____ are lawful for me, but all things _____ _____."

5. "By _____ Noah . . . prepared an _____ to the saving of his house."

6. "Let all _____ be done unto _____."

7. "Give none _____, neither to the Jews nor to the _____ nor to the _____ of _____."

8. "But take heed lest by any means this _____ of yours become a _____ to them that are _____."

9. "For meat destroy not the _____ of God. All things indeed are _____ but it is _____ for that man who eateth with _____."

BRIEF ANSWERS

Define these words:

1. Expedient _____
2. Edify _____
3. Specified _____
4. Substitute _____
5. Lawful _____
6. Offend _____

TALK TIME — DISCUSSION

1. By reading 1 Corinthians 6:12 and 1 Corinthians 10:23 we learn that an expedient must first be lawful.

   a. How can we know when a thing is lawful? _____
   _____

   b. Does a thing have to be mentioned specifically to be lawful? _____ If not, how is it authorized? _____

   c. Be prepared to show that a thing which is unlawful (not authorized by God) cannot be expedient. _____

   d. Discuss the expression "but I will not be brought under the power of any" (1 Cor. 6:12; cf. New American Standard Bible and New King James Bible). What does this mean? _____
   _____

   e. Give an example of an unlawful thing that is thought by some to be an expedient. _____

2. Be prepared to tell the difference between an expedient and a thing that is specified.

   a. What choice does man have regarding

i. The kind of music in Christian worship? _____
   ii. The action of baptism? _____
   iii. Scope of the oversight of elders? _____
   iv. The kind of organization of the church? _____

3. Show that expediency involves the right of choice within the realm of those things which God has authorized.

   a. God authorized gopher wood for the ark. What was Noah's choice as to the kind of wood? _____ As to the tree to use? _____

   b. God authorized unleavened bread for the Lord's table. What choice does man have? _____

   c. God authorized assembling. Where? _____
      For how long? _____

4. Read 1 Corinthians 10:23 and 1 Corinthians 14:26. A scriptural expedient must edify. What does this mean? _____
   _____

5. For a thing to be expedient it must not offend a brother (1 Cor. 10:32).

   a. What about a matter that is specified, can we apply the same rule to it? _____ If not, why not? _____
      _____

6. Be ready to show that an addition to God's word or a substitution for God's way cannot be an expedient. Cite an example. _____
   _____
   _____

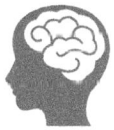 **THINK! "THINK ON THESE THINGS"**

1. Every command of God authorizes whatever is necessary to the carrying out of that command. The Lord says, "Preach the gospel." He specifies WHAT is to be preached—the gospel—but He does not tell HOW to preach it, so we must decide the best methods of preaching.

This is where expediency comes in. While the Lord does not specify how the gospel is to be preached, He does specify WHO is to do the preaching—the church. Thus, He specifies the organization and what is to be preached, but leaves the method to us.

Question: Is the Missionary Society a method of preaching, or must it choose a method? THINK! _____

2. The Lord commanded baptism. The action is specific—a burial—but the place for baptism is not specified. This is where expediency comes in.

    a. Is a baptistery an expedient? THINK! _____

    b. Is sprinkling an expedient? THINK! _____

 **WHAT YOU SHOULD LEARN FROM THIS LESSON**

1. An expedient must first be lawful.

2. An expedient must edify.

3. An expedient must not offend a brother's conscience.

4. An expedient cannot be specified.

5. An addition to God's Word or a substitution for God's way is not an expedient.

Lesson 17

Expediency – Lawful and Unlawful

INTRODUCTION

1. In the last lesson we studied "expediency," noting that to be expedient a thing must first be lawful, must edify, must not offend a brother, and cannot be specified.
2. We should learn how to make a practical application of this lesson or it will be of no profit unto us.
3. On the following page there is a chart of things lawful and unlawful. This chart should help the student to learn how to apply the lesson on expediency.

I. Things Lawful
   A. These things are authorized in God's word.
      1. Authority may be established in one of three ways:
         a. Direct statement or command
         b. Approved example
         c. Necessary inference
      2. Authority may be either generic or specific.
         a. Generic authority makes everything in that realm lawful.
         b. Specific authority makes the thing specified lawful and all other things in that general realm are unlawful.
      3. In the realm of things lawful some things will be specified and others will be expedients.
         a. If there is no authority for them, they are unlawful and cannot properly be labeled as expediencies.

II. Things Unlawful
   A. These are things which are not authorized in God's Word.
      1. Things for which there is no generic or specific authority

B. These things are sinful regardless of what we think of them or how much we may think they facilitate the work of the Lord.
    1. If there is no authority for them, they are unlawful and cannot be properly labeled as expediencies.

III. Study the Chart on the Following Page
   A. The following Scriptures authorize the ten (10) items listed under "Lawful: Specified" (matters of faith).
      1. Hebrews 10:25; James 2:2; Acts 20:7; 1 Corinthians 14:23
      2. Matthew 28:19; Mark 16:16; Acts 2:38
      3. Ephesians 5:19; Colossians 3:16
      4. 1 Corinthians 16:1-2; 2 Corinthians 9:6-7
      5. Mark 16:15-16; 2 Timothy 4:1; 1 Timothy 3:15
      6. Matthew 26:26-30; Luke 22:18, 29-30; Acts 20:7
      7. Acts 2:44; 4:32-35; 11:29; Romans 15:25-31; 1 Corinthians 16:1-2; 2 Corinthians 8:4; 9:1, 12; 1 Timothy 5:16
      8. Matthew 28:20; 2 Timothy 2:2; 4:1-2
      9. Galatians 6:6; 2 Corinthians 11:8; 1 Corinthians 9:14
      10. Acts 20:28; 14:23; 1 Peter 5:1-4

LESSON 17 Expediency – Lawful and Unlawful

LAWFUL		UNLAWFUL
SPECIFIED	**EXPEDIENT**	**NO AUTHORITY**
1. **Assemble**	Place: rent, own, buy, build? Sit or stand; heat or cool; light	
2. **Baptize**	Where? baptistry, river Water: cold or warm? still or running? fresh or salt water?	Sprinkling, pouring Babies or unbelievers "Because of" remission
3. **Sing** Psalms, hymns, and spiritual songs	Books or memory? Number of songs? Sit or stand?	Instruments of music Choir
4. **Lay by in store** Who? Every one of you When? First day of week How? As God prospers	Cash or check? In basket or hat? Beginning or end of service?	Raffling matches Chicken dinners Business enterprise Investments
5. **Preaching** What? Gospel of Christ Who? Disciples Organization? Church	When? How? Where? Anytime Pulpit, radio, TV, tract? Private or public?	Another doctrine Missionary society Colleges
6. **Drink this cup** What? Cup When? First day of week Where? In the kingdom Who? Every disciple	Fermented or unfermented? Morning or evening? How served? One container or many?	Coffee, tea, Coke Thursday night, once a year Outside the kingdom For "priest" only
7. **Relieve the needy** Who? Needy saints	Money, food, clothing Provide facilities	Benevolent society, orphan home, old folks home, another gospel, another organization
8. **Teach** Who? The taught	Arrangements: time, place, size of group	To refuse to support Beg public donations
9. **Support of preacher** What? Support Whom? Laborer	How it is given: money, house, food, utilities Frequency	Sprinkling, pouring Babies or unbelievers "Because of" remission
10. **Jurisdiction of elders** Where? Local church	How they oversee, the number and frequency of meetings, teachers used	One elder Assume oversight of members, monies, work of another church

Lesson 18

Expediency – Lawful and Unlawful (Questions)

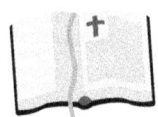 **WHAT DOES THE SCRIPTURE SAY?**

References: Heb. 10:15; Mark 16:15; Eph. 5:19; 1 Cor. 16:1-2; Matt. 26:26-28; 2 Cor. 8:4; 9:1; Matt. 28:20; 1 Cor. 9:14; 1 Pet. 5:1-4

1. "Not _____ the assembling of _____ together, as the manner of some is."

2. "Go ye into all the _____ and _____ the _____ to every creature."

3. "Speaking to yourselves in _____ and _____ and spiritual songs _____ and making _____ in your heart to the Lord."

4. "Upon the first day of the _____ let everyone of you _____ by him in store, as _____ hath _____ him."

5. "And he took the _____, and gave thanks, and gave it to them saying _____ ye all of it."

6. "And take upon us the _____ of ministering to the _____."

7. "Teaching them to _____ all things whatsoever I have _____ you."

8. "Even so hath the _____ ordained that they which _____ the gospel should live of the _____."

9. "Feed the _____ of God which is _____ you, taking the oversight thereof."

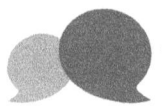

TALK TIME — DISCUSSION

1. By what authority can the church build a meeting house? Read Hebrews 10:25.
   _____
   _____

2. Why is it scriptural to build a baptistery but wrong to practice sprinkling? _____
   _____

3. What is the difference between having song books and using a piano since neither are mentioned in the New Testament? _____
   _____

4. What are some matters of expediency in regard to our giving? _____
   _____

   a. Why are dinners and raffling matches, etc. wrong? _____
      _____

   b. Is how we raise money for the work of the church a matter of choice? _____

5. If the Missionary Society sends out men to preach the gospel, what could be wrong with it? _____

   a. Is it the preaching that is wrong? _____ Or the organization? _____

   b. Since some colleges teach the Word of God, would it be right for churches to make contributions to them? _____ If not, why not?
      _____

6. We reject Thursday night communion, but we use individual containers for the Lord's Supper. Why? _____
   _____

   a. What makes the first wrong? _____

   b. Why is the latter right? _____

LESSON 18 Expediency – Lawful and Unlawful (Questions)

7. What are some expedients in the work of relieving the needy saints? _____

   a. What are some unlawful things? _____

   b. Why are they unlawful? _____

8. Be prepared to show that Bible classes are expedients. _____

9. Discuss the supporting of the preacher. _____

   a. What are some expedients in this? _____

   b. Can you read in the Bible of churches furnishing houses for preachers? _____

10. Can you read in the Bible where the elders of one church became the "sponsors" of the work of many churches? _____

THINK! "THINK ON THESE THINGS"

1. Is the Bible class arrangement, as we have it on Sunday mornings, a matter of faith or choice? THINK! _____ Would it be right to have a Sunday School Organization? _____ Why? _____

2. When a church furnishes a house for a preacher, does this put the church in the real estate business? THINK! _____

3. Over whom do the elders have the oversight? The local church? Is the number of elders a matter of choice? What about having only one elder? THINK! _____

4. If the elders of one church have proven ability in the management of money, can other churches turn over part of their money to these elders? THINK! _____

5. Since we have electric lights, air conditioning, toilets, P.A. systems, and cry rooms in our building, none of which are mentioned in the Scripture, are we doing things for which there is no authority? THINK!

6. If it is scriptural to have rest rooms and water fountains, why not have a kitchen and dining room? THINK! _____
   _____

   Why are some things which are not mentioned in the Scripture acceptable and other things are not? THINK! _____
   _____

TRUE OR FALSE

1. An expedient would be anything we think is helpful in doing God's will. _____

2. All expedients have been specified in the Scripture. _____

3. Expediency involves the right of choice in the realm of those things which God has authorized. _____

4. No expediency should be forced to the offending of a brother's conscience. _____

5. If a thing is expedient, it need not be lawful. _____

6. A thing that is specified cannot be a matter of expediency. _____

7. The command of God authorizes everything required to carry out that command. _____

8. God forbids the church owning its meeting house. _____

9. Whether or not a church supports a preacher is a matter of choice. _____

10. The instrument of music in worship is an aid just like the song book. _____

11. The church may build and maintain any kind of organization which the elders feel will facilitate the work of the church. _____

LESSON 18 Expediency – Lawful and Unlawful (Questions)

12. There is just as much authority in the Bible for sprinkling as there is for a baptistry. _____

13. Whether or not the church relieves the needy saints is a matter of choice. _____

14. Whether or not a church makes a contribution to a college is a matter of expediency. _____

15. The number of churches that come under the oversight of an eldership is a matter of choice. _____

 **WHAT YOU SHOULD LEARN FROM THIS LESSON**

1. To distinguish between things specified and things expedient
2. That expediencies may not be mentioned in the Scripture
3. That unlawful things are never expedient

Lesson 19

Authority and the Silence of the Scripture

INTRODUCTION

1. What should be our attitude toward the silence of the Scripture? Does the silence of the Scripture on any subject give liberty to men to engage in that thing? What should we do regarding those things about which the Lord says nothing?
2. These are questions of importance, the answers to which will go a long way toward settling differences that exist. These questions have to do with one's attitude toward the Word of God. Every one has an attitude toward the Scripture, but it may not be the right attitude.

I. Two Attitudes Toward the Silence of the Scripture

   A. Statement of these attitudes
      1. Where the Bible is silent, where God has not spoken, we are at liberty to act as we think best. Thus, silence gives freedom to act.
      2. Where the Bible is silent we must be silent. We can do only those things which the Lord authorized.
   B. These different attitudes were prevalent in the Reformation Movement.
      1. Martin Luther, the great German reformer, felt that we were at liberty to do anything not expressly forbidden.
      2. Ulrich Zwingli, the great Swiss reformer, felt that only that which is expressly authorized should be taught or practiced
   C. These attitudes were present during the Restoration Movement of the nineteenth century.
      1. The expression "We speak where the Bible speaks and are silent where the Bible is silent" was a famous expression during the early nineteenth century.
         a. Compare: "If any man speak, let him speak as the oracles of God" (1 Pet. 4:11).

       b. Those who held forth this claim felt that we could do only that which God authorized.
    2. Later, some misinterpreted this expression and began to teach, "Where the Bible is silent we have liberty," i.e., freedom, to act.
  D. These attitudes were involved in the division of the nineteenth century.
    1. Those who came to be known as the Christian Church (Disciples of Christ) adopted the view we speak where the Bible speaks; where the Bible is silent we have liberty, freedom to act as we think best.
       a. This explains why they accepted the missionary society and mechanical instruments of music, even though neither is authorized in the New Testament.
          i. Later they had state-wide organizations, trained choirs, "fellowship-halls," chicken dinners, ice cream socials, women preachers, etc. on the same grounds, i.e., the Bible doesn't say not to have them, or the silence of the Scripture.
          ii. They contended that the Lord told us to preach the gospel, but He did not say how, so we can use the missionary societies. They argue that the Lord did not say not to use the instrument.
    2. Churches of Christ continue to believe, "Where the Bible is silent we are silent."
       a. They rejected both the societies and instruments of music on the grounds that they were not authorized in the Scripture.
  E. In this generation these attitudes prevail.
    1. Many members of churches of Christ are now accepting the view of the Christian Church of years past concerning the silence of the Scripture.
       a. They institute various programs and promotions and are unable to give scriptural authority for them.

- b. The cry has gone forth, "We do many things for which we have no authority."
  - i. They must believe the silence of the Scriptures permits their doing these things, i.e., church suppers, social affairs, recreational activities, brotherhood-wide projects, sponsoring churches, missionary societies (without calling them missionary societies), benevolent societies (without calling them benevolent societies), unwed mothers' homes, youth camps, etc.
- 2. Others continue to believe and preach, "Where the Bible is silent, we are silent."
  - a. We believe there must be authority from God before we can teach or practice a thing.

II. Does the Silence of the Scripture Authorize Anything?
  A. God must reveal Himself unto man.
    1. All that we know about the will of God is that which God has revealed (1 Cor. 2:9-11).
      a. We cannot know the mind of God by His silence; thus, silence does not authorize anything.
      b. We cannot know whether God will be pleased with anything we do unless He has revealed His will on that thing. Examples:
        i. We know God is pleased when we worship Him in Spirit and in truth, for He has revealed this unto us (John 4:23-24).
        ii. We know what God wants the church to do—preach the word, edify the saints, and care for its needy—for He has revealed this unto us (Eph. 4:8-12).
        iii. We do not know that God is pleased when the church provides entertainment and recreation, for He has not revealed this unto us.
          a. It is presumptuous to conclude that God is pleased when the church sponsors entertainment just because those entertained are pleased.

B. An example of the silence of the Scripture
   1. Moses "spake nothing concerning" priests coming from the tribe of Judah (Heb. 7:14).
      a. Are we to conclude that, since God is silent about this, priests from the tribe of Judah are acceptable?
         i. If so, Jesus could have been a priest on earth, for He was of the tribe of Judah.
         ii. But Jesus could not be a priest on earth (Heb. 8:4).
         iii. Therefore, when God specifically mentions Levi as the priestly tribe and says NOTHING about other tribes, they are prohibited from being priests.
   2. Silence does not give consent! Silence prohibits!
      a. We are not to think of men above that which is written (1 Cor. 4:6; cf. 2 Pet. 1:3; 2 Tim. 3:16-17).
      b. We must act with authority from Christ, doing all in His name (Col. 3:17).
      c. Where the Scriptures stop, our teaching and practice must stop.
C. Some things which are practiced under the guise of "The Silence of the Scripture"
   1. Burning of incense in worship
      a. There is nothing morally wrong with burning incense, but it cannot be done as a religious act, for the Lord has not authorized it. Though the New Testament is silent on it, this silence does not give liberty to practice it.
   2. Sprinkling for baptism
      a. The New Testament is silent on sprinkling for baptism. The Lord does not say, "Thou shalt not sprinkle," but He specifies what to do—baptize, bury (Rom. 6:3, 4).
   3. Mechanical instruments of music in worship
      a. The Lord is silent on this subject; just as silent as He is about priests from the tribe of Judah, He says nothing about instrumental music in worship.

b. God specifies the kind of music for Christians—singing (Eph. 5:19; Col. 3:16).

c. Instruments of music are not wrong as such, but in worship to God they are just as unscriptural and unauthorized as priests from the tribe of Judah.

4. Missionary societies, benevolent societies, human institutions or organizations other than the local church doing the work of the church

   a. The Lord specifies the organization of the local church (Acts 14:23; Phil. 1:1; Rom. 16:16).

   b. He is as silent about missionary societies and benevolent societies as He is about priests from the tribe of Judah. His silence does not authorize them.

   c. Some of these societies, as educational societies and benevolent societies, medical societies, etc. have their place, just as washing of hands, burning of incense and instruments of music have their place. BUT THAT PLACE IS NOT IN THE CHURCH OF THE LORD.

5. Extended oversight of the elders of a local church

   a. God restricted the work of elders to "the flock which is among you" (1 Pet. 5:1-3; Acts 20:28).

   b. The Scripture is silent about elders overseeing two or more churches, their work, members, or money. But this silence does not justify elders of one church assuming the oversight of another church or any part of its work.

CONCLUSION

1. We must respect what God says, but we must also respect what He does not say. Our attitude toward the silence of the Scripture is important.

Authority and the Silence of the Scripture (Questions)

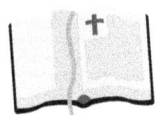 **WHAT DOES THE SCRIPTURE SAY?**

References: 1 Cor. 4:6; 2 Pet. 1:3; Col. 3:17; Rev. 22:18; Heb. 7:14; Heb. 8:4; 1 Cor. 2:9-13; 1 Pet. 4:11

1. "And these things, brethren, I _____ in a figure transferred to _____ and Apollos for _____ _____; that you might learn in us not to think of _____ above that which is _____."

2. "According as his divine power hath given unto us _____ _____ that pertain unto _____ and _____, through the knowledge of him that hath called us to glory and virtue."

3. "And whatsoever ye do in word or deed, _____ _____ in the name of the _____ _____ giving thanks to God and the Father by him."

4. "For I _____ unto every man that heareth the words of the _____ of this _____, if any man shall _____ unto these things, God shall add unto him the plagues that are written in this book."

5. "For it is evident that our Lord sprang out of _____; of which _____ Moses spake nothing concerning priesthood."

6. "For if he were on earth, he should not be a _____, seeing that there are _____ that offer gifts according to the law."

7. "For what man knoweth the things of a man, save the _____ _____ of man which is in him? even so the _____ of _____ knoweth no man, but the _____ of God. Now we have

received, not the spirit of the world, but the spirit which is of God; that we might _____ the things that are freely given to us by God."

8. "If any man speak, let him speak as the _____ of _____."

BRIEF ANSWERS

1. What is meant by the silence of the Scripture? _____
   _____
2. Are we given the liberty to add unto the teaching of God's Word? ____
3. By what authority must all things be done? _____
4. How can we know the mind of God? _____
5. Has God revealed His complete will for mankind? _____

TALK TIME — DISCUSSION

1. There are two prevailing attitudes toward the silence of the Scripture. Be prepared to discuss these attitudes (Refer to outline, point I.).
   _____
   _____
2. What was the basic difference between the thinking of Martin Luther and Ulrich Zwingli with regard to the silence of the Scripture? ____
   _____
3. What famous expression, concerning the silence of the Scripture, prevailed during the early nineteenth century? _____
   _____
   a. Do you know who first made this statement? _____
   b. How does it compare with 1 Peter 4:11? _____
   _____

LESSON 20 Authority and the Silence of the Scripture (Questions)

4. Discuss the different attitudes toward the silence of the Scripture which were manifested in the division in the nineteenth century. _____
   _____

   a. What attitude was taken by those known as the Christian Church?
   _____

   b. How did those in the churches of Christ continue to feel? _____
   _____

5. Upon what basis did brethren try to defend the missionary society and the instrument of music? _____
   _____

   a. Did they set forth the scriptural authority for such? _____

   b. If not, how did they attempt to defend them? _____
   _____

6. After the missionary society and instruments of music, what other things were brought into the practice of those brethren under the silence of the Scripture? _____
   _____
   _____

7. The writer of Hebrews says, "Moses spake nothing concerning" the priests of the tribe of Judah (Heb. 7:14). What conclusion is then reached concerning priests from this tribe? _____

   a. Is this an example of the silence of the Scripture? _____

   b. Does the silence of the Scripture give liberty to act in realms unauthorized? Or does it prohibit such? _____

   c. Does silence give consent? _____

8. Be prepared to show that the silence of the Scripture does not authorize the burning of incense in worship, sprinkling for baptism, and instrumental music in worship _____

   a. Was the Lord as silent about these things as the law was about priests of the tribe of Judah? _____

9. Is the Scripture silent about churches building missionary societies, benevolent societies, education societies, medical societies, and social centers? _____

    a. Does this silence authorize churches to build and maintain any of these? _____

    b. Are these morally wrong? _____

10. Who is responsible to preach the gospel? _____
    What is the only organization of the church? _____

THINK! "THINK ON THESE THINGS"

1. The only way man can know the mind of God is when God has revealed it unto us (1 Cor. 1:9-13). If God has not revealed His will on a given subject, either in a generic or specific way, how can we know that He would be pleased if we do that? THINK! _____

    a. Has God revealed His will regarding the work of the church? THINK! _____

    b. Is it presumptuous to conclude that God will be pleased because we are pleased with a given project? THINK! _____

    c. Are we at liberty to do any and every thing that God has not expressly forbidden? THINK! _____

2. Moses, in the law, speaks nothing about priests of the tribe of Judah. The law taught that priests were to be of the tribe of Levi. When God specifies the tribe of Levi this excludes, or leaves unauthorized, all the other tribes, and God's silence about priests from the tribe of Judah does not give liberty to appoint them as priests. His silence does not authorize anything. With this thought in mind think on these things:

    a. God specifies the kind of music in worship. Does this prohibit, or leave unauthorized, the use of any other kind? THINK! _____

    b. God specifies the acts of Christian worship. What does this prohibit, or leave without authority? THINK! _____

LESSON 20 Authority and the Silence of the Scripture (Questions)

    c. God specifies the action of baptism. What does this prohibit, or leave without authority? THINK! _____

    d. God specifies the organization of the church. What does this prohibit, or leave without authority? THINK! _____

    e. When God specifies the realm of the oversight of elders, what does He prohibit, or leave without authority? THINK!_____

 **WHAT YOU SHOULD LEARN FROM THIS LESSON**

1. God authorizes in a generic and specific way. Generic authority includes everything in that realm, but specific authority excludes, or leaves unauthorized, everything but that which is expressly formulated. Thus, a thing does not have to be specifically mentioned to be authorized or expressly forbidden to be unauthorized.

2. We know the mind of God only as He has revealed it unto us.

3. We are not at liberty to add unto or take from that which God has revealed.

4. The silence of God does not authorize anything.

5. We must have authority, either generic or specific (established by a command, an approved example, or necessary inference) before we act.

Lesson 21

Authority and Evangelism

INTRODUCTION

1. Having learned in past lessons the need for authority, that there are two sources of authority—God and men, that there are two kinds of authority—generic and specific, that authority is established in one of three ways—direct command, approved example, and necessary inference, we should recognize our need for authority in the realm of evangelism.

I. The Church Is to Engage in the Work of Evangelism

   A. Authority for such a work
   Note: Perhaps none would question the fact that the church should be busy in the work of evangelism, but we should be able to establish authority for such.

      1. A direct statement (1 Tim. 3:15).

         a. The church is "the pillar and ground of the truth."

            i. She is the foundation and support of the truth; she holds up and displays the gospel to the world. This is the major work of the church.

      2. An approved apostolic example

         a. The Jerusalem church sent Barnabas to Antioch (Acts 11:22).

         b. The church at Philippi had fellowship with Paul in the gospel (Phil. 1:3-5).

         c. The church at Thessalonica "sounded out the word of the Lord" (1 Thess. 1:8).

II. How the Church Did Its Work of Evangelism

   A. Individuals went out (Acts 8:4; 5:42; 8:5; 9:22, 29).

      1. Each Christian has a responsibility to teach the word to the best of his ability, and to increase his ability to teach. The

emphasis in the New Testament is upon the individual, but the church as a unit (local church) has a responsibility apart from that of the individual.
   2. In the local church there should be teaching designed to instruct and encourage personal evangelism.
B. The local church and evangelism
   1. How the church did this work
      a. The local church supported a gospel preacher (1 Cor. 9:14; 2 Cor. 11:8).
         i. He may be supported while he preaches in that area since he is worthy of his hire and should live of the gospel. Though Paul did not allow Corinth to support him while he was there, he later asked them to forgive him of this wrong (cf. 2 Cor. 12:13).
         ii. The Jerusalem church sent Barnabas to Antioch (Acts 11:22).
      b. The local church may support a man while he preaches in another area.
         i. Philippi had fellowship in the gospel with Paul (Phil. 1:3-5; 2:25; 4:14-18). They sent to Paul at Thessalonica (4:16) and at Rome. The book of Philippians was written from Rome. Paul had received "the things which were sent" from Philippi by their messenger Epaphroditus (4:18; 2:25).
      c. Several churches may support the same preacher (2 Cor. 11:8-9).
         i. Brethren in Macedonia supported Paul while he was at Corinth.
         ii. More than one church sent unto him. This is church cooperation in the support of a preacher.

2. A study of the pattern.
    a. Things found in the pattern
        i. Each church gave as it could.
        ii. Each church sent directly to the preacher.

PATTERN

```
C ─╮
C ──────────────▶ preacher
C ─╯
```

    b. Things not found in the pattern
        i. No church ever sent money TO another church for preaching. Money was always sent directly to the preacher.
            a. Someone says, "What difference does it make?"
            b. ONE BIG DIFFERENCE—one is in the New Testament but the other is not. If not authorized, it cannot be right.
        ii. No church ever sent money THROUGH another church for preaching.
            a. Agency destroys equality and brings subordination.

NOT IN THE PATTERN

3. Notice how some are doing it today: Many churches send to one church, which is known as the "sponsoring church"; the elders of this church oversee the work, i.e., selecting the preacher, the field of work, etc., while the other churches furnish the money.

      a. The organization may be scriptural—no organization but the local church—but the function of that organization is unscriptural. No church can scripturally function as a brotherhood agency in preaching the gospel.

      b. Each church bears the same responsibility to preaching the gospel, i.e., preach it to the best of its ability. The church with 500 members would preach the gospel to the best of its ability, but so should the church of 50 members.

      c. There is no authority—either generic or specific—for a "sponsoring church" in the work of evangelism. In the absence of authority such an arrangement cannot be scriptural.

  4. The missionary society and the sponsoring church

      a. The missionary society is a perversion of organization.

         i. It is an organization apart from the church which exists without divine authority.

      b. The sponsoring church is a perversion of the function of the church.

         i. It does a brotherhood work (preaching the gospel) and oversees brotherhood funds.

         ii. God restricted the elders to the local church (cf. 1 Pet. 5:1-4; Acts 20:28; Acts 14:23).

CONCLUSION

1. We have noted that the church in the apostolic days engaged in the work of evangelism.

    a. The local church may support a gospel preacher.

    b. The local church may send out a man to preach in another city.

    c. Many churches may send to the same preacher.

       i. Note: In the New Testament the church sent directly to the preacher. There was never another **organization** standing between the church and the preacher: There was never another **church** standing between the church that sent and the preacher who received support.

2. Since we emphasize "speaking where the Bible speaks and being silent where the Bible is silent" we should follow the New Testament pattern of preaching the gospel or forfeit our claim and suffer the penalty.

Authority and Evangelism (Questions)

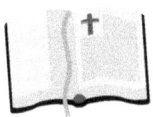 **WHAT DOES THE SCRIPTURE SAY?**

References: 1 Tim. 3:15; Acts 11:22; Phil. 1:3-5; Phil. 2:25; Phil. 4:15;
1 Thess. 1:8; Acts 8:4, 5; Acts 9:22, 29; 1 Cor. 9:14; 2 Cor. 11:8, 9; Acts 20:28;
1 Pet. 5:1-4

1. "But if I tarry long, that thou mayest know how thou oughtest to behave thyself in the _____ of God, which is the church of the _____ _____, the pillar and ground of the truth."

2. "And they sent forth Barnabas that he should _____ as far as _____."

3. "I thank my God upon every remembrance of you . . . for your _____ in the _____ from the first day until now."

4. "Yet I supposed it necessary to send to you _____, my brother, and companion in labour, and _____ _____, but your _____ and he that ministered to my wants."

5. "Now ye Philippians know that in the beginning of the gospel . . . no church _____ with me as concerning _____ and _____ but ye only."

6. "For from you _____ out the _____ of the _____."

7. "Therefore they that were scattered abroad went everywhere _____ the word."

8. "But Saul increased the more in strength, and _____ the Jews which dwelt at Damascus, proving that this is very Christ."

9. "And he spake boldly in the _____ of the _____ Jesus."

10. "Even so hath the Lord ordained that _____ which _____ the _____ should live of the gospel."

11. "Take heed therefore unto yourselves, and to all the _____, over the which the Holy Ghost hath make you _____."

12. "Feed the flock of God which _____ _____ _____, taking the oversight thereof."

BRIEF ANSWERS

1. Does the church have a work of evangelism? _____

2. What means of authority can you cite to establish the fact that the church is to preach the gospel? _____

3. What constitutes the pattern God gives regarding the local church and its work of evangelism? _____

4. What organization is involved in the work of evangelism in apostolic times? _____

5. Has God told us how the church did its work of evangelism? _____

6. Is there a difference between the individual and the church in the work of evangelism? _____

TALK TIME — DISCUSSION

1. Be prepared to discuss the direct statement that shows that the church has a work of evangelism. _____

2. There are examples of New Testament churches doing the work of evangelism. Be prepared to cite these examples.

    a. _____

    b. _____

    c. _____

LESSON 22 Authority and Evangelism (Questions)

3. Discuss the local church sending out a gospel preacher.

   a. Which church serves as an example of this? _____

   b. What preacher did they send? _____

   c. Can a local church today select and send out a man to preach the gospel? _____

4. The local church may support a preacher while he preaches in another city.

   a. Give an example of this from the New Testament. _____

   b. May we do this today? _____

5. What passage shows that several churches may send to the same preacher at the same time to supply his support? _____

   a. May this be done today? _____

6. Discuss how the church sends to the preacher in the New Testament pattern. _____

   a. Name the things found in the pattern and the things not found in the pattern. _____

7. Be prepared to show the difference between how the New Testament churches did the work of evangelism and how some churches of today are doing it. _____

8. What is a sponsoring church? _____

   a. Did they have "sponsoring churches" in the work of evangelism in the apostolic days? _____

   b. Show how a "sponsoring church" perverts the function of the church. _____

c. Discuss the difference between the "sponsoring church" and the Missionary Society. _____
_____

TRUE OR FALSE

1. The New Testament is a complete and perfect guide. _____
2. We must have authority for everything we do. _____
3. There are several examples of sponsoring churches in the New Testament. _____
4. In the New Testament examples, there is never an organization between the church supplying the money for gospel preaching and the preacher. _____
5. The churches of the New Testament did their work of evangelism without missionary societies or sponsoring churches. _____
6. The church is still sufficient in organization to do the work of evangelism. _____

THINK! "THINK ON THESE THINGS"

1. A local church may send out a preacher; it may support a preacher either at home or in another area; it may send to a preacher at the same time other churches are sending to him. Is there any other scriptural way (how) the local church can do its work of evangelism in so far as supporting a preacher is concerned? THINK! _____
2. How does each church bear the same relationship to gospel preaching? THINK! _____
_____
Since each church has the same relationship to gospel preaching, if one church turns over its money to another church for this work, does it become subordinate? THINK! _____

LESSON 22 Authority and Evangelism (Questions)

3. In the absence of a direct command, approved example, or necessary inference for one church sending TO another church to preach the gospel or sending THROUGH another church to preach the gospel, is there any scriptural authority for such a practice? THINK! _____ Is the New Testament a complete and perfect guide? THINK! _____

4. Would it be any greater sin to pervert the organization of the church than it would be to pervert the function of the church? THINK! _____ Would it be any worse to pervert the worship than to pervert the function of the local church? _____ THINK!

WHAT YOU SHOULD LEARN FROM THIS LESSON

1. The church may support a preacher while he preaches in that community or in another area.
2. Several churches may support the same preacher.
3. One church never sent money TO another church to support a preacher.
4. One church never sent money THROUGH another church to support a preacher.

Lesson 23

Authority and Edification

INTRODUCTION

1. When souls are converted, they must not be forsaken and left to wander back into sin. They must be taught how to worship God, how to live a new life in Christ. They must be edified or built up in the most holy faith.
2. "Edification" is defined as: "the act of building; this is used only figuratively in the N.T., in the sense of edification, the promotion of spiritual growth." The verbs "edify" and "edifying" are "used metaphorically, in the sense of edifying, promoting the spiritual growth and development of character of believers, by teaching or by example, suggesting such spiritual progress as the result of patient labour" (W.E. Vine, *An Expository Dictionary of New Testament Words*).
3. One of the last commandments Jesus gives is "teaching them to observe all things whatsoever I have commanded you" (Matt. 28:20).
4. Paul calls this the work of "perfecting the saints" (Eph. 4:12).

I. The Church Is To Engage in the Work of Edification
   A. Authority for this work
      1. Direct statement
         a. To the church at Corinth Paul writes, "when ye come together . . . let all things be done unto edifying" (1 Cor. 14:26).
         b. Paul teaches that the church (body) is sufficient unto the "edifying of itself in love" (Eph. 4:16).
      2. Approved example
         a. While there is no example of a full program of teaching in the local church, there is an example of the church coming together for the purpose of edification (1 Cor. 14:26).
            i. Although this meeting concerns the use of spiritual gifts, still all things were to be unto edifying. Certain gifts were forbidden on the grounds that such would not edify, i.e., speaking in tongues if no interpreter were present (vs. 27-28).

       b. There are examples of teaching being done to the church (those already converted) for the purpose of edification (Acts 2:46; 4:23-30; Acts 11:26).

II. There Were Teachers Set in the Early Church for the Purpose of Edification
   A. God set teachers in the early church (1 Cor. 12:28).
      1. In the beginning miraculous gifts were needed to provide adequate teaching in the church.
      2. Teachers were set in the church for the purpose of teaching those who had been converted. These teachers had miraculous powers, given by the laying on of the apostles' hands, and thus taught by inspiration.
   B. When Jesus ascended to heaven He gave gifts unto men (Eph. 4:7-16).
      1. The gifts were apostles and prophets, evangelists, pastors, and teachers.
      2. The purpose of these gifts
         a. Apostles and prophets for the revelation of divine truth (cf. Eph. 3:5; 1 Cor. 2:12-13; John 16:13)
         b. Evangelists for the propagation of the truth revealed. Example are Stephen of Acts 7 and Philip of Acts 8 (cf. Acts 21:8), Timothy, Titus, Barnabas, and others.
         c. Pastors (elders) and teachers for the work in the local church
            i. Paul declares that we have such gifts "that we be henceforth no more children . . . but speaking the truth in love, may grow up into him in all things, which is the head, even Christ" (Eph. 4:14-15).
            ii. Elders must be men with ability to teach (1 Tim. 3:2; Tit. 1:9-11). They are to "feed the flock" (1 Pet. 5:2), but the flock is to feed upon the Word of God (1 Pet. 2:2; 2 Pet. 3:18); therefore, elders must be able to teach the Word.
         d. Paul says these gifts are given for "the perfecting of the saints," which is the work of teaching in the local church; "for

the work of the ministry"—minister means service, so this is the work of benevolence—and "for the edifying of the body of Christ," which is building up or making larger the body of Christ (church), which is done by gospel preaching.

III. How the Church Did Its Work of Edification (Teaching)
  A. The church is to edify itself (Eph. 4:16).
    1. God has so organized the church that it is able to do its work of edification.
    2. What ever is necessary for the work of edification is authorized in the authority to do this work (Place – Provisions – Personnel).
  B. The church has the authority to recognize the various stages of physical, mental, and spiritual development through which people pass and to arrange teaching for these groups.
    1. People pass through various stages of development: physical, mental, and spiritual.
      a. Some **physical** classifications
        i. Young men and aged men (Titus 2:2, 6)
        ii. Young women and aged women (Titus 2:3-4)
        iii. Children and parents (Eph. 6:1-4)
        iv. Husbands and wives (Eph. 5:22-25)
        v. Masters and servants (Titus 2:9; Eph. 6:5, 9)
      b. Some **mental** classifications
        i. Adults and children—their thinking and understanding differ (1 Cor. 13:11; 14:20).
      c. Some **spiritual** classifications
        i. "Babes" in Christ (1 Pet. 2:2; Heb. 5:12-14)
        ii. "Full age" (Heb. 5:12-14; 1 Cor. 3:2)
    2. Various groups are to be taught according to ability to receive.
      a. God gives material (food) to be taught to the different groups.
        i. "Milk" for babes (1 Pet. 2:2)

ii. "Strong meat" for those who are of full age (Heb. 5:12-14)
     b. Sometimes teaching is withheld because people are not able to bear it.
        i. Jesus had many things to say unto the disciples (apostles) but he says, "Ye cannot bear them now" (John 16:12).
        ii. Paul did not feed the Corinthians with meat, "for hitherto ye were not able to bear it" (1 Cor. 3:2).
     c. Other evidence of classification
        i. Aged men teach certain things, aged women other things (Titus 1:1-8).
        ii. Aged women are to teach young women, but women are not to teach "over the man" (1 Tim. 2:11-12); therefore, some arrangements must be made for this teaching to be done.
        iii. In the early church there were women who prophesied (1 Cor. 11:5), but when the "whole church" was "come together in one place" for edification, the women were to keep silent (1 Cor. 14:23, 34). Therefore, women prophesied at some time and place other than when the whole church came together in one place (assembly) (a necessary inference).
3. There is no legislation on HOW, WHERE, or WHEN these groups are to be taught.
   a. Since the church is to "edify itself," the obligation of teaching rests upon the local church.
   b. God has authorized the work and left the means and methods of accomplishing the work up to us.
   c. Note: God specifies the organization—the church—that is to select the best means and methods available to do the work.
4. The local church may make arrangements to teach these various groups.

LESSON 23 Authority and Edification

      a. Note: If the group arrangement is ruled out, it must follow that all teaching must be done when the whole church is come together. But there were women teachers (1 Cor. 11:5), and they were not to teach over men (1 Tim. 2:11-12); therefore, some arrangement for teaching was made in addition to the general assembly of the whole church.

C. That which is necessary for teaching
  1. **Place** where teaching may be done
  2. **Time** when teaching is to be done
  3. **Persons** who are to teach and those to be taught
  4. **Arrangements** of those who are to be taught

  Note: There is no New Testament limitation or restriction as to place, time, or arrangements or persons who may be taught. Therefore, the elders may arrange whatever is best in view of existing circumstances.

D. The local church under its elders may
  1. Provide the **place** for edification (building, whether rented or owned).
  2. Provide the **personnel** for teaching (teachers).
  3. Provide all necessary **provisions** for edification (group students according to ability, age, or spiritual development, supply materials, etc.).

HOW IT IS DONE

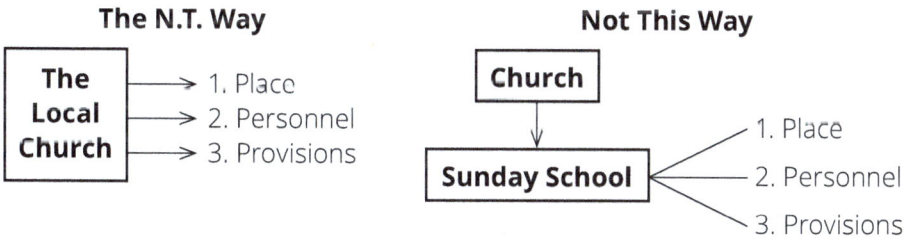

Note: There is no organization but the local church in the work of edification which God gives the church to do. There is no "Sunday School" apart from the local church. While the Bible classes conducted on Sunday may be referred to as a "Sunday School" since they constitute a school conducted on Sunday, they do not constitute another organization but must be conducted under the supervision and oversight of the elders of the church. No class should seek to function in the realm of evangelism or benevolence as a "class" apart from the local church such as in making contributions to certain works or sponsoring certain "projects" or raising money, etc. There is no organization but the local church. Nothing larger, nothing smaller.

IV. The Work of the Church in Edification Does Not Involve Secular Education

   A. The church is to teach the gospel of Christ, the Word of God. It is the pillar and ground of the truth (1 Tim. 3:15).

      1. The place, facilities and personnel which the church provides for teaching is provided to teach the Word of God.

   B. Many churches have gotten into the field of secular education as a business.

      1. There are church sponsored and supported Kindergartens, Elementary Schools, High Schools, and Colleges. These exist in many places across the country and offer a complete curriculum, as public school systems do, and also conduct Bible classes. Since Bible is included in their curriculum, they claim a right to church support. However, churches cannot support such works without also supporting the secular education, sports activities, etc.

      2. The churches of the New Testament never engaged in secular education. The need for education was as great then as now. The need of "Christian environment" was as great then as now. But the apostles did not authorize such a work for the church. The work of the church is preaching the Word, edifying itself, and caring for its needy. There is absolutely no authority from the Lord for the church to engage in secular education. Therefore, those who are involved in such work are doing it solely upon the authority of men.

Note: Remember, there are only two sources of authority—God and men.

CONCLUSION

1. That the church has a work in the realm of edification is accepted by all.

2. The Lord has restricted **what** the church is to teach, i.e., the Word of the Lord, and has restricted the **organization** that is to do the work, i.e., the local church, but has not restricted the time or place or persons to be taught and arrangements for teaching them (cf. Chart Lawful—Unlawful, Lesson No. 17).

3. Let the church do its work of edification, but keep it free from making contributions to secular schools or colleges and from getting into the school business.

Lesson 24

Authority and Edification (Questions)

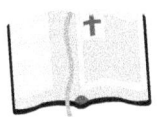 **WHAT DOES THE SCRIPTURE SAY?**

References: Matt. 28:20; 1 Cor. 12:28; 1 Cor. 14:26-33; 1 Pet. 2:2; 5:2; 2 Pet. 3:18; Heb. 5:12-14; Eph. 4:8-16; Acts 11:22-26; Eph. 3:3; 1 Cor. 1:12, 13; Titus 2:1-10; 1 Cor. 13:11; 1 Cor. 11:5; 1 Tim. 2:11-12; Eph. 6:1-4

1. "Teaching them to _____ all things whatsoever I have _____ you."

2. "And God hath set some in the _____, first _____, secondarily _____, thirdly _____."

3. "How is it then, brethren? when ye come together . . . Let _____ things be done unto _____."

4. "As newborn _____ desire the sincere _____ of the _____ that ye may grow thereby."

5. "But _____ in grace, and in the _____ of our Lord and Savior Jesus Christ."

6. "For when for the time ye ought to be _____, ye have need that one teach you again which be the first principles of the oracles of God; and are become such as have need of _____ and not of _____."

7. "For everyone that useth _____ is _____ in the word of righteousness: for he is a _____."

8. "But _____ _____ belongeth to them that are of _____ _____, even those who by reason of use have their senses exercised to discern both good and evil."

9. "And he gave some _____; and some _____ and some _____; and some _____ and _____."

10. "From whom the whole . . . maketh increase of the _____ _____ unto the _____ of itself in love."
11. "And it came to pass that a whole _____ they assembled themselves with the _____ and taught much people."

BRIEF ANSWERS

1. What must we teach unto those who have been converted? _____
   _____
2. Is the local church to engage in the work of edification? _____
3. What means of authority may be cited to show that the church has a work of edification? _____
   _____
4. Define edification. _____
   _____
5. Who is responsible for feeding the local church? _____
6. Is the church sufficient in its organizations to do its work of edification? _____
7. Has the Lord restricted the means and methods to be employed in the work of edification? _____

TALK TIME — DISCUSSION

1. Read Ephesians 4:8-16. Be prepared to discuss the following questions in class.
   a. The gifts that were given unto men, what were they? _____
      _____
   b. What was the purpose of giving these gifts? _____
   c. How long were these to last (Note adverb "till" in verse 13.)? _____
      _____

LESSON 24 Authority and Edification (Questions)

2. In the beginning of the church "God hath set some in the church." Who were they (See 1 Cor. 12:28.)?

   a. Are they the same as the gifts in Ephesians 4? _____

3. What are "pastors"? _____

   a. What is their work in the church? _____

   b. Is their work restricted to the local church? _____

   c. How do you know? _____

4. Ephesians 4:16 makes it evident that the church is to edify itself.

   a. Has God given sufficient organization to the church for this work? _____

   b. What is it? _____
   _____

5. Does God recognize various stages of development of man? _____

   a. What three realms of development does this lesson discuss? Name some classifications in each of these realms.

   i. _____ ii. _____ iii. _____

   _____ _____ _____

   _____ _____ _____

   b. May the church recognize these stages of development and arrange teaching for the different classifications? _____

   c. How should the elders, who are to feed the flock, determine what is to be taught to various groups? _____
   _____

   d. Was the teaching of some truth ever withheld from certain persons? _____ Why? _____
   By whose authority? _____

6. Is there any legislation on how, when, or where the work of edification is to be done? _____

    a. Does this mean the church can choose the how, when, and where? _____

7. Name the three things necessary for the work of edification (While more than three things could be named, restrict it to three things that will cover the field.).

    i. _____ ii. _____ iii. _____

    a. Is the local church capable of providing these necessary things? _____

8. Discuss the church providing secular education.

    a. Do the Scriptures authorize the church to engage in secular school business? _____

    b. On what basis do some seek to justify the church providing secular education? _____

    c. Is the need for "Christian Education" and "Christian Environment" any greater now than it was in the first century of the church? _____

THINK! "THINK ON THESE THINGS"

1. Since the church is to edify itself but the Lord has not specified the means and methods for such a work, does this leave the local church free to select the means and methods that seem best in view of existing circumstances? THINK! _____ If the church can select the means and methods for the work of edification, can it also select another organization to do this work? THINK! _____

2. The elders are charged to "feed the flock of God which is among you." Does this mean that the elders must do all the teaching in the flock? THINK! _____ How can the elders determine who are capable of teaching? THINK! _____

    May they arrange a special class for training teachers? THINK! _____ Should the elders know what is being taught in the various classes? THINK! _____

LESSON 24 Authority and Edification (Questions) 127

3. Several men, each of whom is a dedicated Christian, build and operate a factory. They determine that each day during the noon hour they will conduct a Bible class for all employees who wish to attend. Since the Bible is being taught every day in their factory, does this authorize the church making contributions to their factory? THINK! _____ Since several employees are Christians, and these Bible classes are helping to edify those Christians, can the local church contribute to the factory on the grounds that the factory is helping to accomplish the work of edification? THINK! _____ If, instead of a factory, these same men start a school and include Bible classes in the curriculum, does this authorize the church making contributions to their school? THINK! _____ Since several of the students of the school are Christians, can the local church contribute to the school on the grounds that the school is helping to accomplish the work of edification? THINK! _____ If you reason that the church could contribute to the school, then why not contribute to the factory, since the Bible was being taught in both places? THINK! _____

WHAT YOU SHOULD LEARN FROM THIS LESSON

1. The church is to edify itself.
2. The church has the authority to recognize the various stages of physical, mental, and spiritual development through which people pass and to arrange teaching for these groups.
3. The church is authorized to provide all necessary things for the work of edification, i.e., place, personnel, and provision.
4. There is no authority for the church to provide secular education for its members or to make contributions to another organization for this work.

Authority and Benevolence

Lesson 25

INTRODUCTION

1. The benevolent work in which the church of the Lord is to engage and the organization which is to do the work has been the center of much discussion in the church in the twentieth century.

2. Since whatever we "do in word or in deed" must be done "in the name of" Christ (Col. 3:17), it is in order that we study the will of Christ concerning the benevolent work of the church. We should have our hearts set upon doing the will of the Lord, whatever that will may be, and not allow prejudice to blind our minds so that we cannot see the will of our Lord.

I. The Church Is To Engage in Benevolent Work

   A. Authority for such a work (Note: Perhaps none would question the fact that the church has a work in the realm of benevolence, but we must be able to establish divine authority for this work.)

      1. A direct statement (1 Cor. 16:1-3; 1 Tim. 5:16)

         a. "Now concerning the collection for the saints, as I have given order to the churches of Galatia, even so do ye . . . them will I send to bring your liberality to Jerusalem."

            i. Paul commands churches to send relief to the church in Jerusalem.

         b. "That it may relieve them that are widows indeed" shows that the church has a responsibility in benevolence.

      2. An approved example

         a. The Jerusalem church cares for its needy (Acts 2:44-45; 4:34; 6:1-8).

         b. The church in Antioch sends to the brethren in Judea (Acts 11:27-30).

         c. Churches in Macedonia, Achaia, and Galatia sent to the church in Jerusalem to supply their need (Rom. 15:25; 1 Cor. 16:1-2).

II. Three Possibilities for Benevolent Work in Which the Church Is to Engage
   A. The church may care for its own needy saints.
      1. The church in Jerusalem, the model church for all the ages, took care of its needy.
         a. There were needy saints from the beginning of the church (Acts 2:44-45).
            i. The brethren are not trying to care for all the poor in Jerusalem, just those in the church, "all that believed." The church did not relieve those of the world (cf. Acts 3:6).
         b. The need continues in the Jerusalem church (Acts 4:32-35).
            i. Money is laid at the apostles' feet, thus a common treasury.
            ii. Distribution is made according to the need, and it is made only among believers. None among them lacked, so they did a good job.
         c. Caring for the widows (Acts 6:1-8)
            i. There was a daily ministration, but some were being neglected.
            ii. The local church was instructed to "look ye out among you seven men . . . whom we may appoint over this business" (Acts 6:3).
            iii. There are three things necessary for the work of benevolence; they are **place**, **provisions**, and **personnel**. The local church supplied these things. There was no organization but the local church.

HOW IT IS DONE

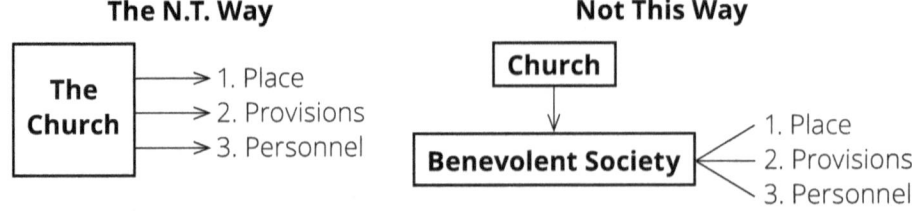

LESSON 25 Authority and Benevolence

Note: Any local church may supply the needs of its saints. In fact the local church is responsible before God to care for its own.

Note: The individual is responsible to care for his own (1 Tim. 5:8) that the church be not charged with such work (1 Tim. 5:16).

B. One church may send to many churches to supply the needs of the saints.

  1. The church in Antioch sends to the brethren in Judea (Acts 11:27-30).

     a. This is the only example in the New Testament of one church sending to many churches; thus, we will do well to study it.

     b. The record says they "sent it to the elders by the hands of Barnabas and Saul." Elders are restricted to the local church; thus, it is necessarily inferred that they sent to the different local churches in Judea where the need existed.

  2. Why did Antioch send to the churches in Judea?

     a. The receiving churches had needy members whose needs they could not supply. This is the only reason for sending funds from one church to another church.

     b. Any local church may send funds to another church or churches when the receiving church has members whose need they cannot supply.

HOW IT IS DONE

Note: There was no organization between the sending church, Antioch, and the receiving churches in Judea. There was no "sponsoring church" between the sending church and the receiving churches. God shows us how one church sends to many churches.

C. Many churches sending to one church
  1. The churches of Macedonia, Achaia, and Galatia sent to the church in Jerusalem (1 Cor. 16:1-3; 2 Cor. 8:1-5; 9:1-2; Rom. 15:25-32).
     a. It is an indisputable fact that many churches sent to the Jerusalem church. Paul had commanded them to send and approved their sending, thus authorizing our doing WHAT they did for the same purpose they did it.
  2. This is the only example of many churches sending to one church. We would do well to observe the REASON for their sending and HOW they sent.
     a. Their reason for sending
        i. The Jerusalem church had members in need of temporal things, the necessities of life, which she was unable to supply.
        ii. Paul commanded these churches to send to Jerusalem "that there may be equality" (2 Cor. 8:13-15), thus the reason for the sending.
           a. Equality does not mean that each church had the same number of members or the same number of dollars, but that there was no need among the saints in any of the churches.
           b. The gathering of the manna in the wilderness serves to illustrate equality: "He that had gathered much had nothing over; and he that had gathered little had no lack." (cf. Ex. 16:16-18).
           c. The churches that sent to Jerusalem had more than those in Jerusalem, but, sometime in the future, they may be in need, and Jerusalem may then supply their need.

b. How it was done
   i. The sending church sent directly to the church in need. There was no organization between the sending church and the receiving church. There was no "sponsoring church" between the sending church and the receiving church.

HOW IT WAS DONE

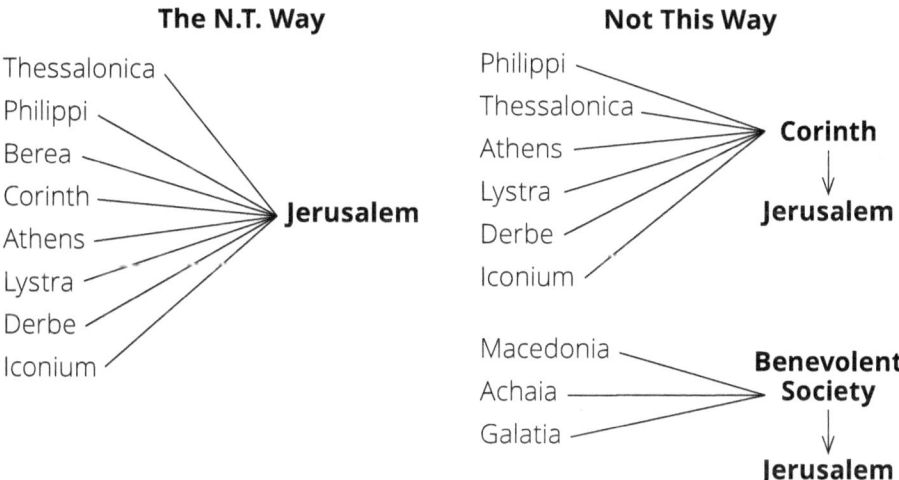

Note: This sending unto Jerusalem is not to be confused with that of Acts 11:27-30, when Antioch sent to the brethren in Judea. Antioch's gift to the churches of Judea had occurred some twelve to fourteen years before this one.

III. The Benevolent Work of the Church Was Unto the Saints
   A. A look at the examples of benevolence
      1. "All that believed" (Acts 2:44-45)
      2. "Them that believed" (Acts 4:32-35)
      3. "The disciples" (Acts 6:1)
      4. "Relief unto the brethren" (Acts 11:29)
      5. "Unto the saints" (Rom. 15:25)
      6. "For the poor saints" (Rom. 15:26)

7. "Accepted of the saints" (Rom. 15:31)
8. "Collection for the saints" (1 Cor. 16:1)
9. "Ministering to the saints" (2 Cor. 8:4)
10. "The ministering to the saints" (2 Cor. 9:1)
11. "Supplieth the need of the saints" (2 Cor. 9:12)
12. "Relieve them that are widows indeed" (1 Tim. 5:16)

Note: There is neither command nor example for the church to engage in a work of general benevolence. We should be content to let the church do the work God gives it to do.

CONCLUSION

1. There are three possibilities of benevolent work of the church taught in the Word of God. God shows us what the benevolent work of the church is and how the churches in the New Testament days did this work, in so far as organization is concerned. Let us do the work God gives us to do in the way He sets forth.
2. Remember that benevolence is not the major work of the church. It is subordinate to the work of preaching the gospel. Let's keep first things first.

Lesson 26

Authority and Benevolence (Questions)

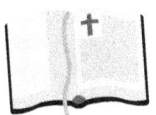 **WHAT DOES THE SCRIPTURE SAY?**

References: Col. 3:17; 1 Cor. 16: 1-4; 2 Cor. 9:1-15; 1 Tim. 5:16; 2 Cor. 8:1-24; Acts 2:44-45; Acts 4:32-35; Acts 6:1-8; Acts 11:27-30; Rom. 15:25-32

1. "And whatsoever ye do in _____ or _____, do _____ in the _____ of the Lord Jesus."

2. "Now concerning the _____ for the _____, as I have given order to the _____ of Galatia, even so do ye."

3. "And when I come, whomsoever ye shall approve by your letters, them will I send to bring your _____ unto _____."

4. "If any man or woman that believeth have widows, let _____ relieve them, and let not the _____ be charged; that it may relieve them that are _____ indeed."

5. "How that in a great trial of affliction the abundance of their joy and their deep poverty abounded unto the riches of their _____. For to their power, I bear record, yea, and _____ their power they were willing of themselves; praying us with much entreaty that we would receive the _____, and take upon us the _____ of the ministering to the _____."

6. "For as touching the ministering to the _____, it is superfluous for us to write unto you."

7. "And all that _____ were together, and had all things common: and sold their possessions and _____, and _____ them to all men as every man had _____."

8. "And the multitude of them that _____ were of one heart and of one soul: neither said anything of them that ought of the things which

he possessed was his own; but they had _____ _____ common."

9. "Neither was there any _____ them that _____; for as many as were possessors of _____ or houses sold them and brought the prices of the things that were sold, and _____ them down at the _____ feet: and _____ was made unto every man according as he had need."

10. "There arose a murmuring of the _____ against the _____, because their _____ were neglected in the daily ministration."

11. "For it hath pleased them of _____ and _____ to make a certain contribution for the poor _____ which are at Jerusalem."

BRIEF ANSWERS

1. Has the Lord given the church a work in the realm of benevolence? _____

2. What means of authority may we cite to establish the fact that the church is responsible to relieve certain needy people? _____
_____

3. What constitutes the pattern God gives us for the work of benevolence? _____

4. There are three possibilities for benevolent work in which the church is to engage. Name these three possibilities. _____
_____

5. Has the Lord showed us how (what organization) the early church did this work? _____

6. Is there a difference between the individual and the church in the work of benevolence? _____ Give one Scripture reference which shows this difference. _____

7. Is the work of benevolence the major work of the church? _____ If not, what is the major work of the church? _____

LESSON 26 Authority and Benevolence (Questions)

8. For whom has God made the church responsible in the realm of benevolence? _____

9. Should the church have a benevolent program as a means of trying to convert the people of the world? _____ What is God's power to convert men? _____

    _____

TALK TIME — DISCUSSION

1. The Jerusalem church serves as a model to all churches in caring for their needy. Be prepared to tell the class how this church cared for its needy (See outline point II.A.). _____

    a. What three things are necessary in doing the work of benevolence? _____

    _____

    b. Did the Jerusalem church provide these things? _____

    c. Can the church today provide these things? _____

    d. Tell one thing the Jerusalem church did NOT do. _____

2. One church may send to many churches. The church at Antioch serves as an example of this truth. Be prepared to tell WHY and HOW the church at Antioch did this work (See outline, point II.B.). _____

    _____

    a. Under what conditions may one church send funds to another church? _____

    b. Show how this work of the Antioch church was NOT done. _____

    _____

3. Many churches may send to one church in a work of benevolence. Study point II.C. of the outline and be prepared to discuss this in class.

    a. Which churches were the sending churches? _____
    Which church was the receiving church? _____

Was this the same as the relief sent to Judea by Antioch (Acts 11)? _____

b. What was the reason for their sending to Jerusalem? _____
_____

c. Discuss "equality" and be prepared to cite the illustration which shows what equality means. _____

d. How did the churches send to Jerusalem? _____

e. Be prepared to tell the class how it was NOT done._____
_____

4. In every instance of benevolent work of the church in the New Testament who were the recipients of the relief? _____

   a. Does this serve as a pattern for the church today? _____

   b. Does the church have divine authority for setting up a program of "general benevolence," i.e., a program to relieve those of the world?_____

THINK! "THINK ON THESE THINGS"

1. There are two sources of authority—divine and human. Divine authority, the New Testament, authorizes the church to care for the needy saints who have no family to provide for them. If the church engages in general benevolence, by what authority does it do it? THINK!_____

2. God has authorized the local church to care for its own. An example is the church in Jerusalem. Does this mean that the church should help to pay or pay the hospital bill for every member who is hospitalized? THINK!_____

3. The New Testament teaches that one church should send to another church when the receiving church has members who are in need and it is unable to supply that need. Does this authorize one church sending to another church for any other purpose such as supporting

a preacher? THINK! Note: We have authority to do WHAT the churches of the New Testament did for the same PURPOSE they did it. _____ Does it authorize a church to set up a program of benevolence that they know they cannot support and beg other churches to send money to them? THINK! _____

4. To learn the will of the Lord on a given subject we must study the Scripture that relates to that subject. Example: We learn the relation of baptism to salvation by studying the passages that mention baptism and salvation. We cannot study those that mention faith and its relation to salvation and learn the relation of baptism to salvation. Question: Can we learn the responsibility of the church in benevolence by studying the passages that deal with evangelism? THINK! _____ Can we learn how churches cooperated in evangelism by studying how they cooperated in benevolence? THINK! _____ Can we apply the principle of one church sending to another church in benevolence, to the work of evangelism? THINK! _____

5. One church sent to another church only when the receiving church had members who were in need of physical things. Does this authorize one church sending to another church for any other reason? THINK! _____

 **WHAT YOU SHOULD LEARN FROM THIS LESSON**

1. The church has a work of benevolence.
2. There are three possibilities for benevolent work
    a. One church caring for its own
    b. One church sending to another church or churches
    c. Many churches sending to one church
3. The work of benevolence was not done by making contributions to benevolent societies.

A Comprehensive Test on Authority

BRIEF ANSWERS

Answer with a brief statement. Each question counts one point.

1. Define authority. _____

2. What questions do the chief priest and elders of the Jews ask Jesus that show they recognize the need of authority and that authority must be from the right source? _____

3. Name an Old Testament example which illustrates the need of authority (one we have studied in this series). _____

4. Give one New Testament reference that teaches the need of authority (one we have studied in this series). _____

5. There are only two sources of authority. What are they? _____

6. Who has all authority in heaven and earth? _____

7. What is the standard of authority in religion today? _____

8. What are the two kinds of authority? _____

9. Before a thing can be expedient it must first be _____

10. Does the silence of the Scripture authorize anything? _____

TRUE OR FALSE

1. We do not need authority for everything we do in religion. _____

2. Generic authority authorizes everything in that general realm, i.e., all of the specifics in that realm. _____

3. Specific authority restricts one to that which is specified and excludes or leaves unauthorized everything else. _____

4. A thing does not have to be expressly stated in the New Testament to be authorized. _____

5. A thing does not have to be expressly condemned in the New Testament to be sinful. _____

6. The work of the church does not include secular education. _____

7. In the New Testament times one church never sent money to another church to enable the receiving church to preach the gospel. _____

8. A "sponsoring church" is frequently mentioned in the New Testament. _____

9. If a thing is not authorized either in a generic or specific sense, we have no right to include it in the worship or work of the church. _____

10. Whatever we do, "in word or deed," must be done "in the name of the Lord" Jesus. _____

11. Getting results is the only thing of importance in arranging the work of the church. _____

12. The church may sponsor various recreation activities if the elders approve of such and feel that such activities will help the local church. _____

13. In New Testament times there was no organization larger than the local church and none smaller than the local church. _____

14. The Lord has given sufficient organization to the church to enable it to do everything he expects of it. _____

15. The elders in the church are restricted in their oversight to the flock of God which is among them. _____

A Comprehensive Test on Authority

 **CHECKING YOUR VOCABULARY**

Match the words on the left to the definitions on the right. One point for each.

1. Unlawful
2. Expediency
3. Generic
4. Authority
5. Approved example
6. Specific
7. Edification
8. Necessary inference
9. Lawful
10. Direct statement

____ things authorized in the Word of God

____ precisely formulated or restricted

____ things which are not authorized in God's Word

____ a statement of fact; a command

____ a necessary conclusion drawn from given data

____ the act of building; the promotion of spiritual growth

____ the right of choice within the realm of things authorized

____ general; opposite of specific

____ an example approved by inspired men

____ legal or rightful power; a right to command to act; dominion; jurisdiction

HOW TO ESTABLISH AUTHORITY

There are three ways of establishing authority. Name these ways and give an example of each. (Five points for each correct answer, fifteen point question.)

Ways of Establishing Authority   **Example**

1. _____   _____

2. _____   _____

3. _____   _____

 **AUTHORITY AND EVANGELISM**

Preaching the gospel is the major work of the church. The church may support a gospel preacher at home or one who is preaching in other areas. Show how churches in the New Testament did this work. Draw a diagram to illustrate "the pattern" and that which is "not in the pattern." (Ten point question.)

The N.T. Way **Not in the Pattern**

 AUTHORITY AND EDIFICATION

After souls are converted, they must be taught how to worship and serve the Lord. This is the work of edification. Though there is no example of the detailed program of edification in the New Testament, we know by direct statement, approved example, and necessary inference that this work was done. Show how it was done, i.e., that which the local church is authorized to do. Draw a diagram which illustrates "The N.T. way" and "not this way." (Ten point question.)

The N.T. Way **Not This Way**

 **AUTHORITY AND BENEVOLENCE**

There are three possibilities for benevolent work in the local church. For each of these possibilities, draw diagrams that show "The N.T. way" and "not this way." (Ten points for each correct answer. Thirty point question.)

1. One church taking care of its own—show how it was done.

    The N.T. Way　　　　　　　　　　　**Not This Way**

2. One church sending to another church or many churches—show how it was done.

    The N.T. Way　　　　　　　　　　　**Not This Way**

3. Many churches sending to one church—show how it was done.

    The N.T. Way　　　　　　　　　　　**Not This Way**

www.ingramcontent.com/pod-product-compliance
Lightning Source LLC
Chambersburg PA
CBHW070448050426
42451CB00015B/3395